FOOD, WINE & SONG
Music and Feasting in Renaissance Europe

FOOD, WINE & SONG

Music and Feasting in Renaissance Europe

Ⓣ Sung Texts / Textes chantés / Gesangstexte / Textos cantados / Testi

Ⓥ Recipes / Recettes / Rezepte / Recetas / Ricette

MANGER, BOIRE et CHANTER

Festins musicaux de la Renaissance

BURGUNDY 1426–c.1490 BOURGOGNE

SPAIN & PORTUGAL c.1480–c.1530 ESPAGNE & PORTUGAL

GERMANY c.1500–c.1585 ALLEMAGNE

THE ORLANDO CONSORT

Robert Harre-Jones *countertenor* Charles Daniels *tenor*
Angus Smith *tenor* Donald Greig *baritone*

"I want to eat, sing and make merry — that's what I like!"

These words come from a 13th-century French song, yet who today could possibly disagree with them? Throughout the ages music and dining have been natural partners, the combination of the two satisfying many of the senses at the same time. Whether it be a grand feast or a small intimate gathering, the choice of an exquisite menu in combination with perfectly selected music has the magic to create an immense feeling of well-being. This anthology of music and recipes has been chosen to give a glimpse of how our distant ancestors might have enjoyed these delights and a very clear picture emerges to indicate that they knew all too well how to have a very good time!

The music presented here was composed over a period of some 350 years. During these years the world witnessed some extraordinary artistic events and achievements: the construction of the great European cathedrals, the flowering of the Renaissance (in painting, sculpture, literature and architecture), the spawning of universities, and the invention of the printing press. The work of medieval and Renaissance musicians was no less remarkable and innovative, and the diversity of style in this collection is a vivid testimony to the inventiveness of composers and, by association, the virtuosity of performers.

The majority of the pieces on this disc are about specific items of food. They take in the different stages of the journey from cultivation to consumption. They tell us of the different contexts for eating, whether it be a picnic, a grand feast or a session at the local inn. And there are times when it becomes all too evident that the texts may purport to be about food but are really about sex.

Other items have been included for their description of topics associated with food, such as etiquette and shopping at the market. Indeed, such songs are very important, for they build up information and answer questions about medieval and Renaissance eating habits that cannot be ascertained from the recipe books alone.

In such a collection it has been impossible to avoid the subject of alcoholic beverages. It is said that beer was not as potent in medieval times as today, and that wine was regularly drunk in watered down form. However, the inescapable conclusion must be that, however weak the drink, intoxication was a regular condition for many of these musical revellers!

FRANCE, c.1220–1363

In these years France may with good reason have claimed to be the world's centre for education and culture. The great University of Paris attracted students from all over Europe to study with men such as Peter Abelard and Thomas Aquinas, and the construction in the city of the majestic cathedral of Notre-Dame in the second half of the 12th century was the inspiration behind the development of the influential school of composition that flourished under the leadership of Leonin and subsequently Perotin.

The monophonic *conductus* (unaccompanied song) **In paupertatis predio** comes from a manuscript compiled at Notre-Dame; the elegant meandering of the melody is stylistically very typical. The unknown poet describes the humble toil of St. Francis of Assisi (1181–1226), telling of how his loving cultivation of vines and figs mirrors his dedication to 'fallen spirits'. The Franciscan order had become firmly established in France by the time of the saint's death, somewhat at the expense of the older orders where the lavish lifestyles of their members contrasted unfavourably with the renouncement of worldly goods by Francis' followers.

Chançonette / Ainc voir / A la cheminee / Par verité is a *motet* dating probably from the end of the 13th century; in the medieval sense this term often referred to songs where each voice sang a different text which may or may not be related to each other. This song—which can be found in manuscripts in Montpellier and Bamberg but which was certainly written in the North of France—combines courtship (the nightingale), unfulfilled love, "salt meat, fat capons... dice and the backgammon board" and a debate on the merits of wine from France and the Rhineland.

Adam de la Halle was one of the most famous *trouvères* of his day (the *trouvère* being the northern French equivalent of the southern *troubadour*). He probably studied in Paris and may have written his pastoral entertainment *Le Jeu de Robin et Marion* for the entertainment of soldiers campaigning in Italy in the service of the Count of Artois around 1282. **Prenés l'abre /**

5

Hé resvelle toi Robin is a song to accompany a picnic scene, many examples of which abound throughout the course of the play. Many foods are evoked and the emphasis is, almost inevitably, on those connoting parts of the body.

Guillaume de Machaut (c.1300–1377) was a poet, the most important composer of his day, and a landmark figure in the development of song. Machaut worked in the service of John of Luxemburg, the King of Bohemia, and John, Duke of Berry, before living his final years in Reims. The enchanting and ecstatic **Nes qu'on porroit** describes the breathlessness of love, but has an unusual and enigmatic connection with food. In a letter from 1363, Machaut tells how "...it is, by God, a long time since I have done anything so good. And the tenors are as sweet as unsalted porridge" ('*papins dessales*')[1]. To compare the tenors (the accompanying parts) to gruel clearly indicates that in the 14th century, if not in Dickens' time (see "Oliver Twist"), the dish was regarded as a great delicacy.

ENGLAND, c.1330–c.1450

By the second half of the 14th century, England's reputation as a musical nation was already well established. Many of the famous choir schools that still flourish today had been founded, and English singers and instrumentalists were generally admired throughout the continent of Europe. It is also known that a huge repertoire of music was composed in England during the 14th and 15th centuries but sadly only a small amount has survived. The loss is not simply due to natural decay; indeed, the biggest 'wastage' occurred during the Reformation, when cathedral and monastery libraries were ransacked on the orders of King Henry VIII. Much of the parchment on which the music was written was 'recycled' as material for lining shoes or wrapping fish, but some of it was used for lining new books and it is by reconstructing the notes from these tomes that musicologists have succeeded in rescuing previously lost pieces.

Apparuerunt apostolis comes from a manuscript that had been at Fountains Abbey. It is likely to have been composed around 1330, but it is not certain that it would have been written at Fountains or even sung there; the Cistercians had a reputation for austerity that would appear to run counter to the 'frivolity' of polyphony. Nevertheless, this did not prevent the monks from

[1]Machaut, *Le Livre du Voir Dit*, ed. Daniel Leech-Wilkinson,
transl. R. Barton Palmer, New York, Garland Press, 1998, pp. 124–5.

earning a reputation of being probably the finest ale producers in the land. The malt house at the Abbey was capable of producing over 2,000 gallons of ale every 10 to 12 days, so one must imagine (and hope) that the intention was to sell to the public rather than consume all the produce 'in-house'! Certainly the tradition of monastic brewing lives on today, especially in Belgium.

Nowell, nowell: The boarës head is a carol that immediately evokes the atmosphere of a grand medieval feast. A *carol* in medieval times would not automatically be a piece about Christmas—the term was used to signify a compositional style (not unlike 'sonata form')—but it was considered to be perfectly acceptable to dance to such music as long as the feet did not leave the floor! The composer, Richard Smert, was rector of Plymtree in Devon from 1435 to 1477.

The final song in the English group is a *canon* or round, **Si quis amat**, from a manuscript now at Cambridge University and dating from the early years of the 15th century. The text appears to be an extract from an extensive section on table etiquette for children in a collection known as *The Babees Book*. Touching on the importance of washing fingers frequently during a meal, desisting from nose-picking at table, avoiding using a napkin for wiping teeth clean and generally eschewing boisterousness, the author concludes by beseeching "sweet children" to become "so expert in courtesy that you may advance yourselves to lasting bliss."

ITALY, c.1390–c.1500

That Italy was the birthplace of the Renaissance has been well documented. The late 14th and early 15th centuries saw the rise of the great family dynasties in such cities as Milan, Ferrara, Padua, Pavia, Bologna and Naples. For the rulers of these 'states' a major part of the pleasure of being in their exalted positions was having the opportunity to display to their rivals and those less fortunate just how magnificently wealthy they were. Patronage of the arts provided the perfect opportunity to do this. Artists and musicians suddenly found themselves in a position where their services were being vigorously sought; in the case of singers and composers (at this

THE ORLANDO CONSORT

time the composers were all, first and foremost, singers!) the best were offered positions in the ranks of the cathedral or chapel choir, and their appointments would have entailed their active involvement in the secular as well as sacred affairs of the court. Nor were these talents only displayed in the residence of the patron, for if the Duke or Prince took to the road, so did the musicians.

Just as the *canon* was very popular in England, so it was for a short period at the end of the 14th century in Italy where the form was known as *caccia*, or chase. **Cacciando per gustar** was composed by Antonio Zachara da Teramo (born c.1350–60, died c.1413) who served as a singer in the Papal chapel in Rome in the first decade of the 15th century before appearing at the chapel of the 'antipope' John XXIII in Bologna in 1412. This *Cacciando* dramatically recreates the sounds of the Italian market place in obscure Roman dialects. The variety of goods enumerated is a clear illustration of the culinary possibilities of the day.

The other three songs in this section, two of which can definitely be associated with the 'carnival' tradition, come from Florence in the last years of the 15th century. There were two specific carnival seasons, one beginning just before Lent and reaching a grand climax on Shrove Tuesday, and a second between May Day and the San Giovanni celebrations on June 24th in honour of the city's patron saint. The earliest songs were very much a street tradition, to be sung during torch-lit processions and when pausing in squares and courtyards. During the reign of the Medici Duke Lorenzo the Magnificent (ruled 1469–1492) the proceedings became much more elaborate and formal; decorations and costumes were added to the poetry and music. **The Canto de' cardoni** (to a text by Lorenzo di Filippo Strozzi) and the **Canto di donne maestre di far cacio** (text by Jacopo da Bientina) ostensibly describe the processes for producing the finest cardoons and cheese respectively. However, the poets clearly rejoice in the possibilities these subjects offer for blatant innuendo and *double entendres!*

Heinrich Isaac, born in the southern Netherlands sometime around 1450, served the Medicis from the mid-1480s until the early 1490s. In return for general musical services and for setting Lorenzo's poetry to music, the Duke supported Isaac handsomely and may have even had a hand in arranging the composer's marriage to Bartolomea Bello, the daughter of a Florentine artisan. Isaac certainly contributed to the *canti carnascialeschi* tradition, but **Donna di dentro / Dammene un pocho / Fortuna d'un gran tempo** is a 'combinative' song, cleverly mixing an existing tune (the famous song *Fortuna d'un gran tempo*) with new material. The obsession with using food as a metaphor for body parts yet again comes to the fore with the line *Dammene un pocho di quella maçacrocha* ('give me a little of that breadstick with a knob on the end), but it has to be said that when it is compared with other songs of the period this could be taken as a model of discreet subtlety!

BURGUNDY, 1426–c.1490

Outside Italy, the most lavish and consistent patrons of music throughout the 15th century were the Dukes of Burgundy. Food and music were inseparable companions at both small and large gatherings and no doubt the party-goers would have enjoyed the fine local wines, produced from vineyards first established by Cistercian monks in the 12th century.

Guillaume Dufay was probably born in or around Cambrai around 1400 and was a chorister at the cathedral there from 1409 to 1412. Before 1420 he must have entered the service of the Malatesta family in Pesaro, Italy, before subsequently holding positions in the mid-1420s in Cambrai and Laon. In 1428 Dufay became a singer in the papal choir in Rome (*see Recipes – Orange Omelette*) and from there went on to establish close associations with the d'Este family in Ferrara and with the court of Savoy. It would appear that from 1440 he was based almost entirely in Cambrai where one of his duties was to be responsible for the *Office du four et vin*, purchasing bread and wine for the whole clerical community, a task one would like to assume he was assigned because of expertise and experience! He died on Sunday 27th November 1474. **Adieu ces bons vins de Lannoys** dates from 1426 and appears to refer to Dufay's own apparently impecunious departure from Laon to Italy, hence the colloquial expression, "I cannot find beans or peas." Nevertheless, such a heartrendingly melancholic song indicates that there was genuine sadness in this leave-taking.

In 1454, Duke Philip the Good held an enormous banquet to raise funds to launch a new crusade to the Orient; the previous year Constantinople had fallen to the Turks. The *raison d'être* of the party, which came to be known as *The Feast of the Pheasant* may have been a solemn and holy cause, but the event was unashamedly lavish and exuberant. The proceedings were described in some detail by Olivier de La Marche: "...*The second table (which was the longest) had a pie in which were twenty-eight live people who, when it came to their turn, played musical instruments... The fourth was a barrel in a vineyard containing two different wines, of which one was sweet and good, the other bitter and nasty; on the barrel was a finely dressed figure holding in his hand a notice saying—Help Yourself* ."* The writer goes on to tell of a 12-year-old boy who rode in on a stag and sang the upper part of a *chanson*, while the stag contributed the tenor.* This was **Je ne vis onques**, thought to be by Gilles Binchois, one of the court's most famous musicians and regarded by many as the most influential song composer of his generation. Sadly no definitive information has survived attesting to the other musical items played and sung at the feast. Nor was a crusade ever launched, but clearly this did not spoil what may have been one of the grandest—and longest—parties in history.

Loyset Compère spent a shorter period of time in service to the Burgundian court than did either Binchois or Dufay; he was probably there in the late 1460s before moving first to Italy, then on to the royal French court and finally to St. Quentin where he died in 1518. **Sile fragor** is a most unusual piece; the poet implores, "Be silent, noise and bustle of the world," so that the music might continue. The writer begs the Mother of God to receive "our hearts, contained in our voices" before finally and whimsically suggesting that it is time to cast out water and have a drink (presumably wine) supplied by Bacchus instead.

There can be no doubt as to the sentiment behind the anonymous **La plus grant chière**; the composer enjoyed the party so much that he simply had to go home and commemorate it in song. If the author is to be believed and the party, held in Cambrai, was audible in Metz then this truly was an epic feat—the distance between the two towns is more than 200 kilometres! Nevertheless, it adds to the body of evidence which suggests that the singers of the day led a hedonistic existence. Documentary evidence from another Burgundian 'possession,' the city of Bruges, shows that on occasion singers were quite willing to be paid not in cash but alcoholic beverages for their services. Moreover, choirs were expected to have collections to fund a

*Olivier de La Marche, *Mémoires*, Book 1, chapter 29. Quoted in translation in "Later Medieval Europe" by Daniel Waley; Longman Publishing, 1964, second edition 1985.

'get-together' for visiting musicians. On one occasion the huge sum raised proved to be too much of a temptation for the singer entrusted with purchasing the food and drink; he ran away and was never seen again!

SPAIN AND PORTUGAL, c.1480–c.1530

Acquiring territory through conquest and marriage, and wealth through the 'development' of lands in South America, the Spanish monarchy came relatively late to the cultural high table of Europe. Stylistically the music—in particular the sacred music—shares many of the characteristics of the other European centres, but gradually the nation shifted from being an importer of compositions to an exporter of composers and singers. Nevertheless, the secular music in Spain always maintained a unique flavour.

La Tricotea, from the *Cancionero Musical de Palacio* is clearly based on the French song *La triquotée*, but turns it, through the neat use of a pun, into a drunken celebration of St. Martin's Day, one of the most important feast days in the European calendar.

Ave color vini clari could almost be regarded as a companion piece to *Sile fragor* (above). The reverent style suggests a pious sacred piece, but it soon becomes clear that this is not an invocation to a holy authority but a comprehensive tribute to the qualities of wine. The composer, Juan Ponce (born c. 1476) was possibly an aristocrat from Andalusia and taught at Salamanca University. Indeed, Ponce's 'solemn' motet, probably dating from around 1495, is an adaptation of a popular student drinking song which in later years was also used by Lassus.

Juan del Encina was born Juan de Fermoselle in Salamanca in July 1468 and died in León in late 1529 or early 1530. Although he was never appointed a member of the Spanish royal chapels, he easily found appointments throughout Spain and travelled to Rome and the Holy Lands. The message of **Oy comamos y bebamos** is readily apparent: eat (plenty), drink (copiously) and be (extremely) merry, for tomorrow we shall all have to 'fast'!

Quem tem farelos is a lively anonymous Portuguese song that shares a heritage with the Italian *Cacciando*; both portray market scenes and the focus in this instance is on the vendors and purchasers haggling for the best possible deal. The song comes from a manuscript in

Coimbra and, like *Oy comamos* is a *villancico*, a term that denotes a piece that alternates verses and refrains. Curiously, just as with the English *carol*, the term nowadays is entirely associated with Christmas carols.

GERMANY, c.1500–c.1585

Perhaps as the result of an extended period of political fragmentation, German music in the Middle Ages remained somewhat isolated until the very end of the 15th century. It was through the emergence of Heinrich Isaac, who after his sojourn in Italy worked for the Emperor Maximilian I, and Ludwig Senfl, a Swiss born musician who began working life as a chorister in the same chapel, that German compositions came to be much more widely disseminated. The two composers, both highly prolific, worked very closely together and in 1513 Senfl took over the leadership of the Imperial *Hofkapelle*. As with so many composers of this period, his serene sacred pieces present a vivid contrast to the lusty secular songs. It is also appropriate, given the reputation of the city of Munich for beer, that Senfl, who spent many years in the city, should write so many splendidly debauched drinking songs, of which **Von edler Art** is but one example.

Mathias Greiter was born in Aichach in Germany around 1494 and died in Strasburg on 20th December 1550. He was an early convert to Protestantism and composed some of the most celebrated tunes and texts of the Reformation but, losing all his positions in the church through a charge of adultery in 1546, he reverted to Catholicism before falling victim to the plague in 1550. **Von Eyren** is an extraordinary song in praise of eggs, yet although it lists all sorts of eggs and all manners of cooking them, it does overlook the omelette recipe created by John of Bockenheim that can be found in the recipe section.

Finally, **Trinkt und singt** is an unfailingly happy anonymous drinking song from a collection compiled by Johann Pühler in Munich in 1585. The message is innocently optimistic: a small drink now and again will do you the world of good and the landlord is such an obliging fellow that he is bound to extend credit until tomorrow!

— ANGUS SMITH / The Orlando Consort

FOOD, WINE & SONG

Initial: Capital V, monk drinking. Sloane 2435 f44v, The British Library.

13

In researching this project, The Orlando Consort has benefited
enormously from the generous help and great expertise provided by
friends and colleagues, including Wyndham Thomas, Daniel Leech-Wilkinson,
David Fallows, Tess Knighton, Leofranc Holford-Strevens,
Susan Weiss and Anne Stone.

The Food

Even the briefest look at a collection of medieval recipes will reveal the ingenuity and creative skills of medieval chefs. But then, perhaps this should come as no surprise. The period covered by this musical anthology was one of great innovation in the food world. With the opening of trade routes to the East, cooks had access to new and exotic spices which could be combined with a staggering array of existing produce. Markets abounded with the freshest produce: vegetables, salads, meat, fish, dairy products, grain and flour, sauces, herbs—the text of *Cacciando* (track 8) provides vivid evidence of this. Moreover, all the produce was organic!

Certainly in preparing medieval recipes one notices a few 'absentees'; potatoes, tomatoes, chillies, the cultivated (as distinct from wild) strawberry and certain types of bell peppers did not arrive in Europe until after the settlement of the Americas. Yet the list of non-available goods is remarkably small and medieval diners would not have lacked for variety.

In truth, not everybody ate 'well' in medieval times; wealth and status accounted for just how lavish a style people lived. There were grand feasts at which the lucky few consumed vast quantities of food over courses too numerous to count and drank obscene volumes of alcoholic beverages. And at the other end of the scale, there were those who subsisted on meagre sustenance and who fell victim through ill-nourishment to plague and other diseases. Yet the 'norm' surely lies somewhere between these two extremes. Medieval cooks were very health-conscious in the preparation of meals, taking great care to offer balanced diets, and were used to working with the ingredients available. This was an age when cooks bought and prepared food according to the season—flexibility and imagination were all-important.

This is reflected by the recipe collections of the day. Most were prepared by chefs at privileged institutions, but while many of the recipes are quite ambitious and lavish, others are extremely simple. The intention would seem to have been to provide ideas suitable for a variety of occasions. In some regards the recipes could be regarded as being quite vague. However, they were not intended to be definitive. Instead, they were regarded as an *aide-mémoire*, assuming that chefs in the home would know the techniques for cooking and would make their own choices as to which herbs and spices to use according to availability and taste. And recipes were sometimes grouped in ways which would be unfamiliar to most modern cooks, the selection being based on what might be suitable for invalids with a variety of 'medieval' diseases, or for clerics who were supposed to observe periods of fasting and abstention.

The dishes included in this anthology have all taken as their starting point recipes that can be found in collections throughout Europe from the 14th and 15th centuries. Some, such as those by Jean-Christophe Novelli, required starting from the drawing board, but others needed very little adaptation. (For example, the Italian section by Rose Gray and Ruth Rogers necessitated only a few changes from recipes they present at the River Cafe). Our modern chefs

have, as their medieval counterparts would have done, combined the texts with their own imagination, but the techniques for cooking and all the ingredients would be recognisable to our ancestors. Wine or beer might be seen as the most suitable accompaniment to all of these dishes—after all, they were probably safer to drink in the Middle Ages than water! And if you want to get a little closer to the medieval 'experience' then we suggest that you eat your meals with spoons and knives only—no mention of forks can be found in English sources before 1463 and they did not come into common usage until the 17th century—but please be aware that resorting to the use of hands would have been considered very poor manners!

— ANGUS SMITH / The Orlando Consort

« Je veux manger, chanter et me divertir, c'est ce qui m'agrée ! »

Ces paroles figurent dans une chanson française du XIIIe siècle, mais qui pourrait y trouver à redire aujourd'hui ? Dans tous les âges, la musique et la table ont été des partenaires naturels, la combinaison des deux satisfaisant simultanément plusieurs sens. Que ce soit dans le cadre d'une grande fête ou d'une réunion intime, l'association d'un menu exquis et d'une musique bien choisie a le pouvoir magique de créer un immense sentiment de bien-être. Cette anthologie musicale et culinaire offre un aperçu de la manière dont nos lointains ancêtres ont pu savourer ces délices, et il apparaît ainsi très clairement qu'ils savaient parfaitement se donner du bon temps !

La musique présentée ici couvre une période d'environ trois siècles et demi durant laquelle le monde connut d'extraordinaires événements et réalisations artistiques : la construction des grandes cathédrales d'Europe, la floraison de la Renaissance (en peinture, sculpture, littérature et architecture), la multiplication des universités et l'invention de l'imprimerie. Les musiciens du Moyen Âge et de la Renaissance ont eux aussi été remarquables et novateurs, et la diversité stylistique de ces pièces témoigne avec éclat de l'inventivité des compositeurs autant que de la virtuosité des interprètes.

La majorité de ces pièces ont trait à des aliments précis. Elles couvrent toutes les étapes qui vont de la culture à la consommation. Elles évoquent divers contextes — un pique-nique, une grande fête ou un repas pris à l'auberge du lieu. Parfois, il ne devient que trop évident que des textes qui prétendent évoquer la nourriture parlent en fait de sexe.

D'autres pièces ont été incluses car leur thème — l'étiquette de la table, les achats au marché — est en rapport avec la nourriture. De telles chansons ont une réelle importance, car elles nous donnent des informations sur les habitudes alimentaires du Moyen Âge et de la Renaissance et répondent à des questions impossibles à résoudre à partir des seuls livres de recettes.

Une telle anthologie ne pouvait éviter le sujet des boissons alcoolisées. On dit que la bière était moins forte au Moyen Âge qu'aujourd'hui et que l'on buvait alors du vin coupé d'eau.

Toutefois, même si les boissons étaient légères, force est de conclure que bon nombre de convives devaient être ivres lors de ces festins musicaux !

FRANCE, v. 1220–1363

En ces années-là, la France pouvait à juste titre se prétendre le centre mondial de l'éducation et de la culture. Des hommes comme Pierre Abélard et Thomas d'Aquin attiraient des étudiants de toute l'Europe à la grande université de Paris, et la construction de la majestueuse cathédrale Notre-Dame dans la seconde moitié du XIIᵉ siècle entraîna le développement de l'influente école de composition qui fleurit sous la direction de Léonin puis de Pérotin.

Le conduit monodique « In paupertatis predio » provient d'un manuscrit compilé à Notre-Dame ; les élégants méandres de la mélodie sont d'un style tout à fait typique. Le poète inconnu y décrit l'humble labeur de saint François d'Assise (1181–1226), l'amour avec lequel il cultive la vigne et les figues reflétant son dévouement envers les « esprits défaillants ». Quand le saint mourut, l'ordre des Franciscains était solidement établi en France, un peu aux dépens d'ordres plus anciens dont le mode de vie fastueux contrastait défavorablement avec le renoncement aux biens terrestres des adeptes de saint François.

Le motet « Chançonette / Ainc voir / A la cheminee / Par verité » date probablement de la fin du XIIIᵉ siècle ; dans son sens médiéval, le terme de « motet » réfère souvent à une chanson dont chaque voix comporte un texte différent, avec ou sans lien l'un avec l'autre. Cette chanson — qui figure en manuscrit à Montpellier et à Bamberg, mais qui fut certainement écrite dans le nord de la France — évoque à la fois la cour (le rossignol), l'amour contrarié, « la chair salée, les chapons gras […], les dés et le jeu de jacquet », un débat sur les mérites comparés des vins français et rhénans.

Adam de la Halle fut l'un des plus fameux trouvères de son temps. Il étudia probablement à Paris et pourrait avoir écrit son pastoral *Jeu de Robin et Marion* pour le divertissement de soldats faisant campagne en Italie pour le service du comte d'Artois vers 1282. La chanson « Prenés l'abre / Hé resvelle toi Robin » accompagne une des scènes de pique-nique dont l'œuvre offre de très nombreux exemples. Elles évoquent divers aliments, qu'elles associent presque inévitablement à diverses parties du corps.

Guillaume de Machaut (1300–1377), poète et compositeur le plus important de son temps, est une figure essentielle dans le développement de la chanson. Il travailla au service de Jean de Luxembourg, roi de Bohème, et de Jean, duc de Berry, avant de revenir à Reims en 1340. Son ravissant « Nes qu'on porroit » évoque les peines de l'amour contrarié. Mais la pièce se rattache elle aussi à la nourriture car, dans une lettre datée de 1363, Machaut écrit : « …Et par dieu lonc temps ha que je ne fis si bonne chose a mon gre. Et sont les tenures [ténors] aussi douces comme papins dessales [gruau dessalé]. » Comparer les ténors (parties d'accompagnement) à du gruau montre clairement que, pour le XIVᵉ siècle et contrairement au temps de Dickens, ce mets était regardé comme très délicat.

ANGLETERRE, v. 1330–c.1450

Vers le milieu du XIVᵉ siècle, l'Angleterre avait acquis une solide réputation de nation musicienne. La plupart des célèbres maîtrises qui y fleurissent encore aujourd'hui existaient déjà, et les chanteurs et les instrumentistes anglais étaient généralement admirés sur tout le continent européen. On sait aussi qu'un immense répertoire musical naquit en Angleterre au cours des XIVᵉ et XVᵉ siècles, mais il n'en subsiste malheureusement qu'une faible partie. Les pertes ne sont pas seulement l'œuvre du temps : les plus grandes eurent lieu durant la Réforme, quand les bibliothèques des cathédrales et des monastères furent saccagées sur l'ordre du roi Henri VIII. Le parchemin « recyclé » servit souvent à doubler des chaussures ou à envelopper du poisson, mais aussi à couvrir des livres, et c'est à partir des textes musicaux conservés par ces volumes que les musicologues ont pu reconstituer des pièces jusque-là perdues.

« Apparuerunt apostolis » provient d'un manuscrit trouvé à Fountains Abbey. La pièce pourrait dater de 1330 environ, mais il n'est pas certain qu'elle ait été composée ni même chantée à Fountains Abbey : de par l'austérité de leurs mœurs, les cisterciens ne pouvaient que condamner la « frivolité » de la polyphonie. Quoi qu'il en soit, les moines gagnèrent néanmoins la réputation de meilleurs producteurs de bière du pays. La malterie de l'abbaye pouvait produire plus de 2 000 gallons de bière tous les 10 à 12 jours, et il faut donc imaginer (et espérer) que c'était dans l'intention de vendre la production au public plutôt que de la consommer « en interne » ! Cette tradition des brasseries monastiques survit encore aujourd'hui, particulièrement en Belgique.

« Nowell, nowell: The boarës head » est un *carol* qui évoque immédiatement l'atmosphère d'une grande fête médiévale. Le *carol* médiéval n'était pas forcément une pièce de Noël — le terme désignait alors un style de composition (qui joua un peu le rôle de la forme sonate au XVIIIe siècle) —, et on considérait qu'il était parfaitement convenable de danser sur une telle musique aussi longtemps que les pieds ne quittaient pas le sol ! Le compositeur Richard Smert fut recteur de Plymtree dans le Devon de 1435 à 1477.

La dernière chanson du groupe anglais, « Si quis amat », est un canon (ou ronde) qui provient d'un manuscrit du début du XVe siècle aujourd'hui conservé à l'université de Cambridge. Il apparaît que son texte est extrait de la longue section que le livre *The Babees Book* consacre à la tenue que les enfants doivent observer à table. Traitant de la nécessité de se laver fréquemment les mains pendant les repas, leur demandant de ne pas se curer le nez à table, de ne pas utiliser la nappe pour se frotter les dents et, de façon générale, d'éviter tout tapage, l'auteur conclut en suppliant les « doux enfants » de devenir « si experts en courtoisie que vous vous élèverez à une félicité durable ».

ITALIE, v. 1390–c.1500

Il a été abondamment montré que la Renaissance naquit en Italie. La fin du XIVe siècle et le début du XVe virent apparaître de grandes dynasties familiales dans des villes comme Milan, Ferrare, Padoue, Pavie, Bologne et Naples. Pour qui gouvernait un tel « État », le plaisir essentiel qu'apportait une si haute charge était de pouvoir étaler son immense richesse devant ses rivaux et devant les personnes moins fortunées. Le mécénat en offrait une occasion idéale. Les services des artistes et des musiciens furent soudain très recherchés ; pour ce qui est des chanteurs et des compositeurs (à cette époque, les compositeurs étaient tous et avant tout des chanteurs !), les meilleurs furent engagés dans les rangs du chœur de la cathédrale ou de la chapelle, et ces

THE ORLANDO CONSORT

nominations devaient les amener à s'engager activement dans les affaires aussi bien mondaines que sacrées de la cour. Et ces talents n'étaient pas seulement exhibés dans la résidence du mécène · si le duc ou le prince prenait la route, les musiciens en faisaient autant.

Si le canon fut très populaire en Angleterre, il le fut aussi pendant une courte période à la fin du XIVe siècle en Italie où cette forme prit le nom de *caccia* (chasse). « Cacciando per gustar » est une œuvre d'Antonio Zachara da Teramo (v. 1350/60–v. 1413), qui fut chanteur de la chapelle papale à Rome dans la première décennie du XVe siècle avant d'intégrer la chapelle de l'« antipape » Jean XXIII à Bologne en 1412. Ce « Cacciando » restitue l'univers sonore d'un marché italien tout retentissant d'obscurs dialectes romains. La diversité des denrées énumérées illustre clairement les possibilités culinaires de l'époque.

Les trois autres chansons de cette partie, dont deux relèvent nettement de la tradition de carnaval, ont été écrites à Florence dans les dernières années du XVe siècle. Il y avait alors deux saisons de carnaval, dont l'une commençait juste avant le carême et culminait le mardi-gras, la seconde allant du 1er mai au 24 juin, jour de la Saint-Jean, célébrée en l'honneur du saint patron de la ville. Les chansons les plus anciennes étaient chantées dans la rue lors des processions aux flambeaux et des stations dans les places et les cours. Durant le règne de Laurent le Magnifique, duc de Médicis qui gouverna de 1469 à 1492, les cérémonies devinrent plus élaborées et plus formelles : des décors et des costumes s'ajoutèrent à la poésie et à la musique. En apparence, le « Canto de' cardoni » (sur un texte de Lorenzo di Filippo Strozzi) et le « Canto di donne maestre di far cacio » (texte de Jacopo da Bientina) décrivent respectivement la meilleure façon de cultiver les cardons et de fabriquer du fromage. Toutefois, le poète goûte visiblement les occasions de sous-entendus et de doubles sens grivois qu'offrent ces sujets !

Né vers 1450 dans le sud des Flandres, Heinrich Isaac fut au service des Médicis depuis le milieu des années 1480 jusqu'au début des années 1490. En remerciement de ses services et pour avoir mis sa poésie en musique, Laurent le Magnifique lui apporta un généreux soutien — il pourrait aussi avoir prêté la main au mariage du compositeur avec Bartolomea Bello, la fille d'un artisan florentin. Si Isaac entretint la tradition des *canti carnascialeschi*, son « Donna di dentro / Dammene un pocho / Fortuna d'un gran tempo » constitue cependant une chanson

« combinatoire » où il mêle habilement airs existants (ici la célèbre chanson « Fortuna d'un gran tempo ») et éléments nouveaux. La propension à faire de la nourriture une métaphore d'une partie du corps apparaît à nouveau dans le vers « Dammene un pocho di quella maçacrocha » (« Donne-moi un peu de ce long gâteau renflé »), mais il faut dire que, comparée à d'autres chansons de l'époque, celle-ci est un modèle de sobre subtilité !

BOURGOGNE, 1426–v. 1490

L'Italie mise à part, les mécènes les plus prodiges et les plus conséquents du XVᵉ siècle furent les ducs de Bourgogne. La nourriture et la musique furent d'inséparables compagnons lors de leurs petites et grandes fêtes, et nul doute que les convives appréciaient les bons vins de la région, issus de vignes mises en culture par des moines cisterciens au XIIᵉ siècle.

Probablement né à Cambrai ou dans ses environs vers 1400, Guillaume Dufay fut enfant de chœur de la cathédrale de cette ville de 1409 à 1412. C'est sans doute avant 1420 qu'il entra au service des Malatesta à Pesaro, Italie, tout en occupant ensuite diverses fonctions à Cambrai et Laon dans le milieu des années 1420. En 1428, Dufay devint chantre de la chapelle papale à Rome (*cf. Recettes — Omelette à l'orange*) et, de là, entretint d'étroites relations avec la famille d'Este à Ferrare et avec la cour de Savoie. Il semblerait qu'à partir de 1440 il ait vécu principalement à Cambrai où, entre autres charges, il eut celle de l'« Office du four et vin » qui consistait à acheter le pain et le vin pour toute la communauté cléricale — on aime à croire qu'elle lui fut confiée pour cause d'expertise et d'expérience ! Il mourut le dimanche 27 novembre 1474. Datée de 1426, la chanson « Adieu ces bons vins de Lannoys » évoque en fait son propre départ de Laon pour l'Italie, l'expression familière « je ne trouve ni fèves ni pois » laissant entendre que ce fut pour cause d'impécuniosité. Quoi qu'il en soit, la déchirante mélancolie de la chanson montre que ces adieux se firent dans une grande tristesse.

En 1454, le duc Philippe le Bon organisa un énorme banquet pour réunir les fonds nécessaires à une nouvelle croisade en Orient — l'année précédente, Constantinople était tombée aux mains des Turcs. Si elle soutenait une solennelle et sainte cause, cette fête restée dans l'histoire sous le nom de « Banquet du Faisan » fut l'occasion de libations et de débordements éhontés.

THE ORLANDO CONSORT

Olivier de La Marche en a laissé une relation assez détaillée : la deuxième table (la plus longue) portait un pâté en croûte dans lequel vingt-huit personnes jouèrent de divers instruments. […] Sur la quatrième, il y avait un tonneau contenant deux vins, dont l'un était doux et bon, et l'autre aigre, avec un écriteau disant « servez-vous ». L'auteur évoque ensuite un garçon de 12 ans qui entra monté sur un cerf et qui chanta le *superius* d'une chanson dont l'animal exécuta le ténor. Il s'agissait de « Je ne vis onques », attribuée à Gilles Binchois, l'un des plus célèbres musiciens de la cour, en qui beaucoup voyaient le compositeur de chansons le plus influent de sa génération. Il ne subsiste malheureusement pas d'informations fiables sur les autres pièces jouées et chantées à cette occasion. Il n'y eut pas de croisade, mais il est clair que cela ne gâcha en rien ce qui dut être l'une des plus grandes — et des plus longues — fêtes de l'histoire.

Loyset Compère resta moins longtemps que Binchois et Dufay au service de la cour de Bourgogne — il y séjourna probablement dans la fin des années 1460. Il se rendit ensuite en Italie, puis à la cour du roi de France et, finalement, à Saint-Quentin où il mourut en 1518. Dans le très inhabituel « Sile fragor », le poète demande au « tumulte du monde » de faire silence afin que les musiciens puissent jouer et chanter. Il supplie la « mère de la divinité » de soutenir « nos cœurs, contenus dans nos voix », puis estime qu'il est temps que l'eau fasse place au vin fourni par Bacchus.

Il ne peut y avoir de doute quant au sentiment qui anime « La plus grant chière » : le compositeur prit tant de plaisir à cette fête qu'il rentra chez lui pour la commémorer par une chanson. À en croire l'auteur, selon lequel la fête de Cambrai s'entendit jusqu'à Metz, l'exploit fut vraiment épique — les deux villes sont distantes de plus de 200 kilomètres ! Toutefois, il y a là une nouvelle preuve du fait que les chanteurs d'alors vivaient en hédonistes. Divers documents conservés à Bruges, autre possession bourguignonne, attestent que les chanteurs acceptaient parfois d'être payés non pas en espèces, mais en bouteilles. Par ailleurs, les chœurs devaient faire des collectes destinées aux « petites réunions » organisées pour les musiciens de passage. Un jour, la somme s'avéra trop tentante pour le chanteur chargé d'acheter la nourriture et les boissons : il s'enfuit et on ne le revit jamais !

FOOD, WINE & SONG

ESPAGNE ET PORTUGAL, v. 1480–v. 1530

Étendant leurs territoires par les conquêtes et les mariages, et augmentant leur richesse par le « développement » de terres en Amérique du Sud, les monarques espagnols vinrent relativement tard à l'art de la table européenne. Par le style, la musique — sacrée, en particulier — a beaucoup de points communs avec celle des autres centres européens, mais d'importateur de compositions, le pays devint progressivement exportateur de compositeurs et de chanteurs. Toutefois, la musique profane espagnole garda toujours une saveur unique.

« La Tricotea », extraite du *Cancionero Musical de Palacio*, dérive clairement de la chanson française « La triquotée » dont elle « traduit » phonétiquement les deux premiers vers en espagnol avant d'enchaîner sur une célébration avinée de la Saint-Martin, l'un des jours de fête les plus importants du calendrier européen.

« Ave color vini clari » pourrait presque être regardé comme un pendant à « Sile fragor » (ci-dessus). Le ton respectueux semble celui d'une pièce sacrée, mais il devient vite clair que, loin d'invoquer quelque sainte autorité, elle rend un hommage détaillé aux qualités du vin. Le compositeur, Juan Ponce (né v. 1476), était peut-être un aristocrate d'Andalousie qui enseigna à l'université de Salamanque. Ce motet « solennel », que Ponce composa probablement vers 1495, est en fait l'adaptation d'une chanson à boire populaire parmi les étudiants, que Lassus reprendra lui aussi.

Né « Juan de Fermoselle » à Salamanque en juillet 1468, Juan del Encina mourut à León à la fin de 1529 ou au début de 1530. Il ne fit partie d'aucune des chapelles royales espagnoles, mais il trouva facilement à s'employer en Espagne et voyagea à Rome et en Terre sainte. Le message de son « Oy comamos y bebamos » est clair : mangeons (abondamment), buvons (copieusement) et soyons (très) joyeux, car demain nous devrons tous « jeûner » !

Comme la pièce italienne « Cacciando », la vive chanson portugaise anonyme « Quem tem farelos » dépeint des scènes de marché, mais elle s'attache plus particulièrement aux marchandages auxquels vendeurs et acheteurs se livrent. Conservée en manuscrit à Coimbra, la chanson est comme « Oy comamos » un villancico, terme qui désigne une pièce alternant couplets et refrain. Curieusement, comme pour le carol anglais, le terme ne désigne plus aujourd'hui qu'un chant traditionnel de Noël.

THE ORLANDO CONSORT

ALLEMAGNE, v. 1500–v. 1585

Peut-être est-ce à cause d'une longue période de morcellement politique que la musique allemande du Moyen Âge resta quelque peu isolée jusqu'à la fin du XVᵉ siècle. C'est avec l'apparition de Heinrich Isaac, qui travailla pour l'empereur Maximilien Iᵉʳ après son séjour en Italie, et celle de Ludwig Senfl, musicien né en Suisse qui commença sa carrière comme enfant de chœur de la même chapelle, que les compositions allemandes commencèrent à se diffuser plus largement. Très prolifiques, les deux compositeurs collaborèrent étroitement, et, en 1513, Senfl prit la direction de la chapelle de la cour impériale. Comme chez de nombreux compositeurs de cette période, il y a un contraste frappant entre la sérénité de ses pièces sacrées et la vigueur de ses chansons profanes. Sans doute est-ce parce que Senfl passa de nombreuses années à Munich, ville réputée pour sa bière, qu'il écrivit tant de chansons invitant si splendidement à la débauche, dont « Von edler Art » n'est qu'un exemple.

Mathias Greiter naquit à Aichach en Allemagne vers 1494 et mourut à Strasbourg le 20 décembre 1550. Il fut l'un des premiers convertis au protestantisme et composa certains des plus célèbres airs et textes de la Réforme, mais, ayant été démis de toutes ses fonctions à l'église suite à une accusation d'adultère en 1546, il revint au catholicisme. Il mourut de la peste en 1550. « Von Eyren » est une extraordinaire chanson à la louange des œufs, mais si elle en énumère une grande variété et toutes les façons de les préparer, elle oublie la recette d'omelette inventée par Johann von Bockenheim qui figure dans la section des recettes.

Pour finir, la joyeuse chanson à boire anonyme « Trinkt und singt » figure dans un recueil compilé par Johann Pühler à Munich en 1585. Le message en est innocemment optimiste : le bon vin ne peut faire que du bien, et l'aubergiste est si obligeant qu'il nous fera crédit jusqu'au matin !

— ANGUS SMITH / L'Orlando Consort

Dans la conduite de ce projet, l'Orlando Consort a largement bénéficié de l'aide généreuse et de la grande expertise d'amis et de confrères parmi lesquels Wyndham Thomas, Daniel Leech-Wilkinson, David Fallows, Tess Knighton, Leofranc Holford-Strevens, Susan Weiss et Anne Stone.

FOOD, WINE & SONG

La nourriture

Il suffit d'un coup d'œil dans un livre de recettes du Moyen Âge pour voir l'ingéniosité et la créativité des chefs de l'époque. Mais il n'y a peut-être pas lieu de s'en étonner. La période que couvre cette anthologie apporta de grandes innovations ; avec l'ouverture de routes commerciales vers l'Orient, les cuisiniers découvrirent de nouvelles épices exotiques. Ils pouvaient les combiner avec les denrées existantes — dont la liste est stupéfiante. Les marchés regorgeaient des produits les plus frais : légumes, salades, viande, poisson, laitages, céréales et farines, sauces, fines herbes — le texte de « Cacciando » (plage 8) le montre clairement. De plus, tous les produits étaient naturels !

Quiconque réalise des recettes médiévales remarquera certainement quelques « absents » : les pommes de terre, les tomates, les piments, les fraises de culture (distinctes de celles des bois) et les poivrons qui n'arrivèrent en Europe qu'après la colonisation des Amériques. Mais la liste en est remarquablement courte, et il est clair que les repas médiévaux ne manquaient pas de variété.

Les plats présentés dans cette anthologie* s'inspirent de recettes indiquées dans des recueils européens du XIVe et du XVe siècle. Si pour certains, ceux de Jean-Christophe Novelli, par exemple, il a fallu tout retrouver, d'autres n'ont demandé que peu d'adaptation. (Les plats italiens présentés par Rose Gray et Ruth Rogers n'ont nécessité que quelques changements dans les recettes qu'elles proposent au River Cafe.) Comme l'auraient fait leurs homologues médiévaux, nos chefs « modernes » ont nourri les textes de leur propre imagination, mais nos ancêtres reconnaîtraient les modes de cuisson et les ingrédients. Ce sont le vin ou la bière qui accompagnent sans doute le mieux tous ces plats — après tout, ils étaient probablement plus sains que l'eau au Moyen Âge ! Et si vous voulez approcher la réalité médiévale d'un peu plus près, nous vous suggérons de ne vous servir que d'une cuillère et d'un couteau — la fourchette n'est pas mentionnée dans les sources anglaises avant 1463, et son usage ne s'est répandu qu'au XVIIe siècle —, mais, de grâce, souvenez-vous qu'il était très mal vu de se servir de ses doigts !

— ANGUS SMITH / L'Orlando Consort

Traduction : Jacqueline Letteron

FRANÇAIS

25

*Voir l'exemple de recette donné page 113. Pour découvrir toutes les recettes traduites en français, rendez-vous sur le **www.harmoniamundi.com**

1 Anonymous, Notre-Dame de Paris

In paupertatis predio
(Solo: Charles Daniels)

In paupertatis predio	In poverty's farm
Franciscus plantat vineam,	Francis plants the vine,
vere vitis propaginem	new production makes
auget nova productio,	the shoot of the true vine grow,
evellens stirpem spineam;	pulling out the thorny stem;
ficus alit dulcedinem,	the fig tree feeds sweetness,
cedit spinetum lilio.	the thornbushes yield to the lily.
In via purgat vitia	On the way he cleanses sins,
corde mundus et opere,	pure in heart and work,
coruscet ut in patria	that he may shine in the heavenly fatherland
culpe liber ab onere.	free from the burden of guilt.
Ad amena pascua	To the pleasant pastures
vagas oves dirige,	guide the wandering sheep;
fac sequi proficua,	make them pursue what is useful,
mentes lapsas erige,	lift up their fallen spirits;
da cum agnis eligi,	grant they may be chosen with the lambs,
da cum granis colligi.	grant they may be gathered with the grain.

FRANÇAIS

Dans sa pauvre ferme, François plante des vignes. Les épines reculent devant les figuiers et les lis. Pur de cœur, il guérit des vices. Guide les brebis errantes vers ces riants pâturages, ranime les esprits défaillants afin qu'ils appartiennent aux élus.

ESPAÑOL

Francisco planta la viña en el erial. Florece la vid y aparta el tallo espinoso; el higo es dulce, los espinos se rinden ante el lirio. Purga los pecados puro de obra y corazón. Brillará libre de culpa. Conduce las ovejas hasta los pastos y levanta su ánimo: serán elegidas con los corderos, serán recogidas con el grano.

ITALIANO

Nell'orto della povertà Francesco pianta uva, fichi, e gigli, che non lasciano spazio alle spine. Nel corso del suo lavoro espia i peccati, per arrivare puro in Paradiso. Porta le pecorelle smarrite ai migliori pascoli, al lavoro utile, ristorandone l'anima nella speranza che vengano scelte tra gli agnelli e raccolte col grano.

DEUTSCH

Auf dem Landgut der Armut pflanzt Franziskus die Rebe, dem Feigenbaum und der Lilie muß der Dornbusch weichen. Auf den Straßen reinigt er von den Sünden. Führe die Schafe auf die saftigen Weiden, ermuntere sie und gib, daß sie auserwählt werden mit den Lämmern und eingebracht mit dem Korn.

2 Anonymous, Montpellier Codex

Chançonette/Ainc voir/A la cheminee/Par verité
(Tutti)

Quadruplum

Chançonette va t'en tost
Au roussignol en cel bois
Di qu'il m'en voist saluer
La douce blonde au vis cler
Et que je l'aim sanz fausser,
Mais certes ne l'os nommer.

Triplum

Ainc voir d'amors n'ai joï,
Si l'ai longuement servi,
N'oncques confort n'i trovai;
Mais quant a li plera,
Ce que servi l'ai
Me sera meri.

Motetus

A la cheminee
El froit mois de genvier
Voil la char salee,
Les chapons gras manger,
Dame bien paree,
Chanter et renvoisier.
C'est ce qui m'agree,
Bons vins a remuer,
Cler feu sans fumee,
Les des et le tablier
Sans tencier.

Tenor

Par verité
Vueil esprover

Quadruplum

Little song, go quickly
to the nightingale in this wood,
bid him go and greet for me
the sweet fair one with shining countenance,
whom I love without playing false
but for sure dare not name.

Triplum

Truly I have had no joy of love,
yet have served him a long time,
and never found comfort in him;
but when it shall please him,
my service to him
will stand to my credit.

Motetus

By the hearth
in the cold month of January
I want to eat salt meat
and fat capons,
[to have] a well-dressed lady,
to sing and make merry.
That's what I like,
good wines for shifting [= drinking],
clear fire without smoke,
dice and the backgammon-board
without quarrelling.

Tenor

In good sooth
I wish to prove

Que vin François
Passent roinnais
Et touz vins aucerrois.

that French wines
surpass Rhenish
and all the wines of Auxerre.*

*Auxerre was not united with the French Crown till 1476; hence its wines are not yet French.

FRANÇAIS
Quadruplum : Chansonnette, dis au rossignol d'aller saluer la douce blonde que j'aime sans oser la nommer.
Triplum : Amour que je sers sans retour me récompensera quand il lui plaira.
Motetus : Près du feu, je veux manger des chapons gras, chanter une belle dame, boire de bons vins et jouer aux dés.
Ténor : Je veux m'assurer que les vins de France surpassent ceux du Rhin.

DEUTSCH
Quadruplum: Kleines Lied, grüß' mir die blonde Schöne, die ich liebe ohne Falsch; doch wage ich nicht, ihren Namen zu nennen.
Triplum: Trost und Freude habe ich noch nicht in der Liebe gefunden, doch wird sie, wenn es ihr gefällt, mir meinen Dienst lohnen.
Motetus: Im kalten Januar am Herd einen fetten Kapaun, ein schmuckes Weib, Wein und Würfelspiel — das ist es, was ich mir wünsche.
Tenor: Führwahr, das will ich beweisen, daß der beste Wein der französische ist.

ESPAÑOL
Quadruplum: Cancioncilla vuela hacia ese ruiseñor y dile que salude a la joven a la que amo.
Triplum: No he tenido alegrías de amor, pero tras servirle largo tiempo tendré mi recompensa.
Motetus: En enero quiero comer carne salada y capones. Tener mujer, cantar, buenos vinos, fuego sin humo, dado y un tablero sin riñas.
Tenor: Quiero probar que el vino francés supera al del Rhin o al de Auxerre.

ITALIANO
Quadruplum: Vai, canzone mia, dall'usignolo: digli che mi saluti la donna che amo con tanta fede, ma che non posso chiamare per nome.
Triplum: Da anni servo Amore, ma da lui non ricevo nè gioia nè conforto; però quando verrà il momento, si ricorderà di me.
Motetus: A gennaio voglio mangiare carne salata e capponi davanti al focolare, con una dama elegante con la quale divertirmi—fuoco senza fumo, e giuochi senza bisticci: così sono contento.
Tenore: Voglio dimostrare che i vini francesi sono migliori di quelli del Reno e di Auxerre.*

*Auxerre appartiene alla Francia solo dopo il 1476, perciò i vini della regione non erano ancora francesi.

3 ADAM DE LA HALLE
Prenés l'abre/Hé resvelle toi Robin
(Angus Smith, Donald Greig)

Cantus
Prenés l'abre Peyronelle
Entre vous et dan Symon,
Si danserons au bedon
Pour l'amour de Marotelle.

Car je voy Gautier Trenelle
Qui aporte une escuëlle
Pour fayre a Marote un don.

Et si voy Henri Cotelle
Qui fayt une sauterelle
Pour danser fort d'un talon.

Avecques luy Tanotelle,
Ysabelle et Marion,
Qui diront une chanson
A la clere fontaynelle
                    Prenés l'abre . . .

Or sus donques, si fretelle,
Robin, de ta charamelle
Et vient a point ton bordon.

Car qui sera la plus belle,
Elle aura la flour nouvelle,
Et uns gans blancs de moton.

Cantus
Take the branch, Péronelle,
between you and Master Simon,
and we shall dance to the drum
for love of Marion.

For I see Gautier Trenelle
who is bringing a bowl
as a present to Marion.

And I see Henri Cotelle
who is doing the 'sauterelle'
dancing with vigour on one heel.

With him are Tanotelle,
Isabelle and Marion,
who will sing a song
beside the clear fountain.
                    Take the branch . . .

Up with you now, Robin,
and play on your pipe,
and your drone comes on cue.

For she who proves the prettiest,
shall have the fresh flower
and a pair of white sheepskin gloves.

Hi ha! que mon cuer sautelle,
Un Robin et Marion,
Basés moy seur le menton
Que no vie est bonne et belle!
    Prenés l'abre . . .

Tenor
Hé resvelle toi Robin
Car on emmaine Marot.

Hey-ho, how my heart's a-leaping!
A Robin and a Marion,
kiss me on the chin,
How good and lovely is our life!
    Take the branch . . .

Tenor
Hey, wake up, Robin,
for they're carrying off Marion.

FRANÇAIS
Cantus : Tenez-vous les mains autour de l'arbre, et nous danserons au son du tambourin. [...] Robin, joue donc de ta cornemuse : ton bourdon vient à point. [...] Que notre vie est bonne et belle !
Tenor : Hé, réveille-toi, Robin, car on emmène Marion.

DEUTSCH
Cantus: Laßt uns tanzen zum Vergnügen Marions. Ich sehe sie vor mir, die Burschen und Mägdlein, wie sie tanzen und singen am Brunnen. Los, Robin, spiel auf der Schalmei, die Schönste soll die Blume haben. Heißa, es hüpft mir das Herz, wie schön ist doch unser Leben!
Tenor: Wach auf, Robin, sie entführen Marion.

ESPAÑOL
Cantus: Toma la rama, Péronelle, y con don Simón bailemos por el amor de Marion. Veo a Gautier Trenelle con una escudilla y a Henri Cotelle que baila sobre una pierna. Con él Tanotelle, Isabelle y Marion que cantarán una canción. Toma la rama... Toca Robin tu flauta y que entre tu bordón. Que quien sea la más bella tendrá una flor y guantes de cordero. Robin y Marion me besan el mentón. ¡Qué hermosa es nuestra vida! Toma la rama...
Tenor: Despierta, Robin, que se llevan a Marion.

ITALIANO
Cantus: Balliamo, Peronelle e Mastro Simone, per amore di Marion, alla quale Gautier Trenelle porta un dono. Già Henri Cotelle balla il saltarello: con lui sono Tanotelle, Isabelle, e Marion, che canterà vicino alla fontana. Forza, Robin, suona il flauto; alla più bella un fiore e guanti bianchi. Mi balla il cuore: Robin e Marion, un bacio—che bella vita!
Tenore: Svegliati, Robin, che rapiscono Marion!

GUILLAUME DE MACHAUT

Nes qu'on porroit

(Robert Harre-Jones, Charles Daniels, Angus Smith)

Nes qu'on porroit les estoiles nombrer
Quant on les voit luire plus clerement
Et les goutes de pluië et la mer
Et la greve seur quoy elle s'estent
Et compasser le tour dou firmament
Ne porroit en penser ne concevoir
Le grant desir que j'ay de vous vëoir.

No more than one can count the stars
when one sees them shining at their brightest,
nor drops of rain and the waves of the sea
nor the sands of the shore along which it stretches
nor measure out the circle of the firmament
could one imagine or conceive
the great desire I have of seeing you.

Et si ne puis par devers vous aler
Pour Fortune qui le veut et deffent
Dont maint souspir me convient estrangler
Quant a vous pense et je sui entre gent,
Et quant je sui par moy secretement,
Adont me fait tous meschies recevoir
Le grant desir que j'ay de vous vëoir.

And if I cannot come before you
by Fortune, who gives and withholds her leave,
wherefore I must smother many a sigh
when I think of you and am in company;
And when I am alone in secrecy
then it makes me suffer every ill,
the great desire I have of seeing you.

Car il me fait complaindre et dolouser
Et regreter vostre viaire gent
Et vo bonté souvereine et sans per
Et la tres grant douceur qui en descent.
Einsi me fait languir piteusement
Mon cuer esprent et estient mon espoir,
Le grant desir que j'ay de vous vëoir.

For it makes me complain and grieve,
and long for your noble countenance,
and your sovereign and peerless goodness
and the immense sweetness that results from it.
Thus it makes me languish pitiably,
seizes my heart and quenches my hope,
the great desire I have of seeing you.

FRANÇAIS

Il est aussi impossible de compter les étoiles
ou de mesurer le tour du firmament que de
concevoir le grand désir que j'ai de vous voir.
La Fortune cependant me le défend. J'étouffe
maints soupirs quand je pense à vous. Car il me
fait languir et perdre espoir le grand désir que
j'ai de vous voir.

DEUTSCH

Ebensowenig wie man die Sterne zu zählen
vermag, kann einer ermessen, wie groß mein
Verlangen ist, Euch zu sehen. Das launische
Glück läßt es nicht zu, und so manchen Seufzer
muß ich unterdrücken. Ich leide Qualen, denn
ich sehne mich so nach Eurer Schönheit,
Anmut und Huld. Ich fühle mich elend, denn
mein Verlangen ist groß, Euch zu sehen.

ESPAÑOL

Como no se pueden contar las estrellas,
ni las gotas de lluvia, ni la arena, no se puede
imaginar mi gran deseo de veros. Y si Fortuna
no me lleva a vos, suspiro en compañía y, solo,
sufro del gran deseo de veros. Pues me lamento
y anhelo vuestra belleza y dulzura. Mi corazón
languidece y se apaga mi espíritu del gran deseo
de veros.

ITALIANO

È impossibile immaginare quanto voglio
vederti—così come lo è contare le stelle, le
goccie di pioggia, le onde e i granelli di sabbia,
o misurare la circonferenza del firmamento.
E se la Fortuna non me lo permette, dovrò
soffrire di nascosto. In assenza della tua nobiltà,
bontà, e dolcezza mi addoloro e mi lamento,
soffro penosamente, e perdo ogni speranza.

5 Anonymous, Fountains Abbey 1st Manuscript

Apparuerunt apostolis v. Spiritus Domini

(Tutti) Polyphonic Verse: Robert Harre-Jones, Angus Smith, Donald Greig

Apparuerunt apostolis dispertite lingue tamquam ignis, seditque supra singulos eorum Spiritus Sanctus. Alleluya.

Spiritus Domini replevit totam domum ubi erant sedentes apostoli.

Seditque supra singulos eorum Spiritus Sanctus. Alleluya

Gloria Patri et Filio et Spiritui Sancto. Alleluya.

(Cistercian Responsory for Whitsun matins)

And there appeared unto the Apostles cloven tongues like as of fire, and the Holy Ghost sat upon each of them. Alleluia.

The Spirit of the Lord filled the whole house wherein the Apostles were sitting.

And the Holy Ghost sat upon each of them. Alleluia.

Glory be to the Father, the Son, and to the Holy Ghost. Alleluia.

FRANÇAIS

Et là apparurent aux apôtres des langues de feu,
et l'esprit du Seigneur emplit toute la maison où
s'étaient assis les apôtres. Et le Saint-Esprit était
sur chacun d'eux. Alléluia. Gloire au Père, au
Fils et au Saint-Esprit. Alléluia.

DEUTSCH

Und es erschienen ihnen Zungen wie von Feuer,
die sich verteilten; auf jeden von ihnen ließ sich
eine nieder. Alle wurden mit dem Heiligen
Geist erfüllt. Alleluja. Ehre sei dem Vater und
dem Sohn und dem Heiligen Geist. Alleluja.

ESPAÑOL

Y sobre los Apóstoles aparecieron lenguas de
fuego, y el Espíritu Santo se posó sobre ellos.
Aleluya. El espíritu del Señor llenó la casa en la
que estaban, y el Espíritu Santo... Gloria al
Padre, al Hijo y al Espíritu Santo. Aleluya

ITALIANO

E apparvero agli apostoli delle linguelle di fuoco
biforcute, e su ciascuna sedeva lo Spirito Santo.
Alleluia. Lo spirito del Signore riempì la casa
dove si trovavano gli apostoli. E su ciascuno
discese lo Spirito Santo. Alleluia. Gloria al
Padre, al Figlio, e allo Spirito Santo. Alleluia.

6 RICHARD SMERT

Nowell, nowell: The boarës head

(Robert Harre-Jones, Charles Daniels, Angus Smith)

Nowell, nowell, nowell, nowell, Noël . . .
Tidingës good I think to tell.[1]

The boarës head that we bring here
Betokeneth a Prince withoute peer,
Is born this day to buy[2] us dear;

Nowell, nowell, nowell, nowell,
Tidingës good I think to tell.

A boar is a sovereign beast
And acceptáble in every feast;
So mote[3] this Lord be to most and least:

Nowell, nowell, nowell, nowell,
Tidingës good I think to tell.

This boarës head we bring with song
In worship of him that thus sprong[4]

Of a virgin to redress all wrong:
Nowell, nowell, nowell, nowell,
Tidingës good I think to tell.

[1] I believe I am telling good news (tidings) / [2] to redeem us at a high price
[3] so may this Lord be to highest and lowest / [4] sprang

FRANÇAIS

Noël, Noël… Je vous apporte de bonnes nouvelles. Cette tête de sanglier présage un prince sans pair, né aujourd'hui pour nous racheter. Le sanglier est une bête digne de figurer dans toutes les fêtes. Nous l'apportons en chantant pour adorer Celui qui est né d'une vierge pour effacer tout le mal. Noël…

ESPAÑOL

Esta cabeza de jabalí anuncia el nacimiento de un Príncipe que nos redimirá. Navidad…
El jabalí es bestia soberana apreciada en toda fiesta. Así sea el Señor en lo bueno y en lo malo. Navidad… Esta cabeza de jabalí traemos con cantos en alabanza del que salió de una virgen para reparar el mal. Navidad…

DEUTSCH

Weihnacht, Weihnacht, frohe Kunde bringe ich euch. Der Schweinskopf, den wir hier bringen, kündet von der Geburt eines Königs; der wird uns erlösen. Ein Schweinskopf ist allzeit willkommen, und so mag auch dieser König der Herr der Höchsten und Niedrigsten sein. Diesen Schweinskopf bringen wir dem zu Ehren, der von einer Jungfrau geboren ist, die Sünde zu tilgen.

ITALIANO

È Natale: vi porto buone novelle. Questa testa di cinghiale vuol dire che è nato un principe senza pari, che ci riscatterà. Il cinghiale è una bestia sovrana, benvenuta ad ogni festa; così sarà il Signore. Cantando portiamo questa testa, per celebrare colui che, nato da una Vergine, correggerà ogni errore.

Si quis amat
(Charles Daniels, Angus Smith, Donald Greig)

Si quis amat dictis absentum rodere vitam

hanc mensam indignam noverit esse sibi.

If anyone enjoys slandering the lives of
the absent,
let him know that he is not fit for this table.

FRANÇAIS
Que celui qui se plaît à dénigrer les absents
sache que cette table n'est pas pour lui.

DEUTSCH
Wenn einer Freude daran hat, Abwesende zu
verleumden, so sagt ihm, daß an diesem Tisch
kein Platz für ihn ist.

ESPAÑOL
A quien ama calumniar a los ausentes hacedle
saber que es indigno de esta mesa.

ITALIANO
Se c'è qualcuno che si diverte a dir male degli
assenti, sappia che questa tavola non fa per lui.

8 ANTONIO ZACHARA DA TERAMO
Cacciando per gustar
(Charles Daniels, Angus Smith, Donald Greig)

Superius

Cacciando per gustar de quel tesoro
per aspri monti e boschi perigliosi,
d'uno boschetto d'alborselli d'oro
de fiuri trova' assai operti e chiusi.
Tastando et odorando i più belli,
et una voce crida
'A li gammarielli
a l'argentarielli
a' lactalini fieschi!
Fieschi, fieschi so' che anche frecciano!
A le telline fieschie!
Tutte giettano la lingua fore!'
'Et so' fieschi quessi lactalini?
Damme derrate dui de gammarielli:
et so' fieschi como dice?'
'A l'infusaglia dolce!'
'O tu da l'uoglio, che bal lu petecto?'
'Voyne cinque.'
'Alle bone melangole,
una ad dinaro!
Costa sei suolli lu centinaro
E buo'ni duy:
Saçço cha fora trista.'
'Se ne buo' tre per duy denari, tolli, tilli.'
'Voil, voil, voil, voil, voil?'

Superius

Hunting in order to enjoy that treasure
through rugged hills and thickets perilous,
in a small clump of golden trees
I found many flowers, open and closed.
(I was) touching and smelling the most beautiful,
and a voice cried out:
'Shrimps,
silverfish,
fresh anchovies!
Fresh, so fresh they're still squirming!
Fresh clams!
They all have their tongues out!'
'And are those anchovies fresh?
Give me two portions of shrimps.
And are they fresh as you say?'
'Sweet lupins!'
'You with the oil, how much for a jugful?'
'I want five.'
'Fine cucumbers,
one for a penny!
A hundred cost six soldi
And I want two;
I know I'll be sorry!'[1]
'If you want three for tuppence, take 'em, keep 'em.'
'Do you want 'em, want 'em, want 'em, want 'em'?

continued on pages 42–43

continued on pages 42–43

[1] Most likely the traditional vendor's 'I'm robbing myself'.

FRANÇAIS

Chassant par les collines, je trouvai des fleurs, ouvertes ou closes. J'entendis des voix crier : « Ah ! les belles crevettes, les beaux anchois ! – Un denier le beau concombre ! Qui veut des cerises ? – C'est fort ! – À qui le tour ? – Qui a de la semoule ? – Et ils sont frais ceux-là ? – C'est combien ? – Voilà, Madame, voilà, j'arrive ! »

ESPAÑOL

Superius: Paseando por un hermoso bosque escuché una voz que anunciaba pescado fresco. "Dame dos porciones de gambas – ¡Altramuces! – Dame diez por un jarro de aceite. – Pepinos – Toma tres por dos denarios. – ¿Quién quiere queso fresco? – No lo es. – ¿Y quién judías? – Ricotta fresca. – Buen aceite, como el ámbar. – Cerezas, higos, melocotones. – ¿Quién duerme, caza y enciende la vela?"

Contratenor bassus: "Mercadería menuda, señora. – ¿Raso, gorgueras, lazos? ¿Mostaza? – Huevos, sémola. – Aceite – Ven, que te despelle-jo. – Ajo, cebollas finas. – Dientes. Quien tiene un mal diente, tiene mal pariente. – Arreglo calderos. – Vinagre como la hiel – ¿Quién quiere husmear? – Señora, voy."

DEUTSCH

Superius: Auf der Jagd fand ich im Wald viele Blumen und roch an einer von ihnen. Da rief eine Stimme: "Garnelen, Sardellen, frische Muscheln! – Sind sie auch frisch? – Ich möchte fünf. – Schöne Pomeranzen, das Stück ein Dinar! – Sardinischer Käse! – Bohnen! – Feine Sauerkirschen! – Frischer Ricotta! – Gutes Öl! – Feigen und Pfirsiche, gekochte Kastanien, meine Dame! – Treten Sie näher! – Wer ist der nächste?"

Contratenor bassus: "Lumpen, Glas, Eisen! – Nadeln, Spindeln, Reste, gnädige Frau! – Mostrich! – Wer hat Eier? – Sind sie auch frisch? – Öl! – Treten Sie näher, wenn Sie in die Zukunft sehen wollen! – Zähne! Schlechter Zahn, schlechte Verwandtschaft! – Wer hat Kessel zu flicken? – Wer will sieben lassen? – Ja, gnädige Frau, ich komme!"

Cacciando per gustar continued from pg.40

'Voyne dare duy?'	'Will you give me two?'
'Chi vuo' li cavalcasi?	'Who wants *caciocavallo*?[1]
Allu caso sardenale,	Sardinian cheese,
allu case della forma,	cheese from the mould,
allu bono latte!'	good milk!'
'No, no no, no, no, no, no.'	'No, no, no, no, no, no, no.'
'Allu bono caso fiescho!'	'Fine fresh cheese!'
'Non è fiescho como dice.'	'It's not fresh as you say it is.'
'Ed è bono, ed è chiaro.'	'It's good and it's clear.'
'E chi vuol le bone schafe?	'And who wants good beans?
E chi le vol le bone visciole?'	And who wants good sour cherries?'
'Alla recotta fiescha!'	'Fresh ricotta!'
'Allo bono oglio,	'Good oil.
como l'unto,	nice and greasy,
più che l'ambra!'	greasier than amber!'
'Alle bone cerase!	'Fine sweet cherries!
E chi le vol le bone ficora?	And who wants fine figs?
E chi le vol le bone perseca?	And who wants fine peaches?
Alle castagne remonne, femmene!'	Boiled chestnuts, ladies!'
'Anna chà, ve' chà,	'Come here, come here,[2]
Famme bene ciò.'	That does me good.'
'È forte.'	'It's strong.'
'Compare, voyme cernere?'	'Good man, do you want to sift for me?'
'Chi altro, chi farina compra, vende	'Who's next, who is buying or selling flour,
'Chi dorme, caccia, stuta e chi accende?'	'Who sleeps, hunts, snuffs the candle, who lights it?'
Contratenor bassus	**Contratenor bassus**
'Ay cinci, ay toppi, ay bretti,	'Rags, tow, glass,
ay ferri, ai rame rotto!'	iron, bits of copper!'

[1]A large round South Italian cheese. / [2]*Anna* is the imperative of *annare* = *andare*, not a proper name

'A l'acora, a le fusa,
alla merciaria menuda, madonna!'
'Chi ha della rasina?
Chi ha frescie o çagane vecchie?'
'Salsa verde, mostarda.'
'Chi ha de l'ova?'
'Chi ha de la semmola?'
'E so' fieschi quessi?'
'A l'uoglio, a l'uoglio!'
'Cy, ci, sta, che scy scortegatu!'
'Vogliune sey suolli.'
'Anna, va for, che te scortiche.'
'No ne vo!'
'Como le day?'
'Voyne dare duy?'
'A l'algli, a l'algli!
Chi le vol le bon cepolle?
'Avante, avante, chi se vo' ciarmare!'
'Chi vol secar li piectene?
Chi vol acconciar piectine da capo?'
'Al dent, al dent!
Chi ha 'l mal dente ha 'l mal parente
e chi ha 'l mal vecino ha 'l mal matino!'
'Chi vol conçar caldare,
centrare e capisteri
e comparare trespidi e copergie?'
'A l'acito, a l'acito, como lo tuosico!'
'Chi vol cernere?'
'Sì maduonna, sì, sallo su!'

'Needles, spindles,
Odds and ends, my lady!'
'Who has any fine satin?
Who has ruffs or old ribbons?'
'Green sauce, *mostarda*.'[3]
'Who has any eggs?'
'Who has any bran?'
'And are these fresh?'
'Olive oil, olive oil!'
'Come here, stand still to be skinned!'
'I want six soldi for them.'
'Come on, out, so I can flay you!'
'I don't want any!'
'What are you selling them for?'
'Will you give two?'
'Garlic, garlic!
Who wants fine onions?'
'Come forward those who want their fortunes
told!'/'Who wants combs cut?
Who wants head-combs mended?'
'Teeth, teeth!
Whoever has a bad tooth has a bad relation
and whoever has a bad neighbour has a bad
morning!'/'Who wants kettles mended,
buckets (?) and tubs,
and to buy trivets and lids?'
'Vinegar, vinegar like gall!'
'Who wants to sift?'
'Yes, lady, I'm coming up!'

[3]May mean mustard, or any of several condiments according to region.

9

Anonymous, Florentine Carnival Song

Canto de' cardoni

(Robert Harre-Jones, Charles Daniels, Donald Greig)

Noi siàn, donne, maestri di cardoni,	Ladies, we are master growers of cardoons,[1]
che ne' nostri orti si fan grossi et buoni.	which in our gardens grow big and good.
Se 'l far, donne, questa arte vi diletta,	If, ladies, you enjoy practising this craft,
benché va di oggidì la cosa stretta,	even though today business is tight,
no' vi darén questa nostra ricetta	we shall give you this recipe of ours,
che non habbiàn da farvi maggior doni.	besides which we have no greater gift to give.
Il modo a culturar un cotal frutto	The way to cultivate such a fruit
è gittar forte il seme per l'asciutto,	is to cast the seed firmly in dry weather
ché quando e' piove, o il seme va mal tutto,	for when it rains, either the seed goes awry,
o produce scrignuti e stran cardoni.	or it produces lumpy and odd cardoons.
Bisogna prima d'intorno sarchiarlo,	First, you must hoe all around,
pigliar le foglie in man et poi legarlo,	take the leaves in hand and then bind it,
coprirlo e ritto ritto sotterrarlo,	cover it, and sow it absolutely straight;
ècci qualcun che lo pianta bocconi.	there are some who plant it lying face down.
Vuol esser il cardon di tal misura,	The cardoon should be in size
un palmo o poco più, che la nattura	a span or a little more, for nature[2]
smaltir non può si gran cosa et sì dura,	cannot digest anything so big and hard,
benché a noi piaccion sempre e' gran bocconi.	even though we always like the big mouthfuls.
Tanto è mangiar il cardon senza sale	Eating an cardoon without salt
quanto far col marito il carnovale,	is like going to carnival with your own husband,
ché 'l sugo per se stesso tanto vale	for the juice by itself is worth as much
quanto alle non pentite le stazioni.	as the Stations of the Cross to unrepentant whores.

[1]The cardoon (Cynara cardunculus) is a relation of the globe artichoke; but it stands throughout for the male organ. / [2]Span: 29 cm; 'nature' in Italian as in Latin also means the (female) sexual organ.

FRANÇAIS

Nous, Mesdames, nous sommes les rois du cardon[1]. Il doit mesurer un pied[2] ou un peu plus, car la nature[3] ne peut digérer de chose si grande et si dure même si nous aimons les grosses bouchées. Manger des cardons sans sel, c'est comme aller au carnaval avec son mari : leur jus vaut autant qu'un chemin de croix pour un mécréant.

[1]Le cardon, genre d'artichaut, est ici une métaphore du pénis.
[2]Le pied mesurait 32,4 cm.
[3]En italien comme en latin, le mot « nature » désigne le sexe de la femme.

ESPAÑOL

Señoras, en nuestro huerto los cardos[1] son grandes y buenos. Si este arte les place les daremos la receta. Deben plantarse en tiempo seco, pues se arruinan con la lluvia. Se desbroza en torno, se toman las hojas con la mano y se entierra muy derecho. La naturaleza no digiere cardos mayores de un palmo[2], aunque nos gusten los grandes bocados. Cardo sin sal es como ir con marido al carnaval, pues su jugo vale tanto como las estaciones a las no arrepentidas.

[1]El cardo (Cynara cardunculus) pertenece a la familia de la alcachofa, pero también alude al órgano masculino.
[2]Palmo: 29 cm; 'naturaleza' en italiano y en latín es también el órgano sexual (femenino).

DEUTSCH

Meine Damen, wir sind Meister der Artischockenzucht[1]. Wenn Sie das Handwerk erlernen möchten, geben wir Ihnen gern unser Rezept. Gesät wird bei Trockenheit, es wird rundum gehackt und dann absolut gerade gepflanzt. Die Größe der Artischocke sollte eine Spanne betragen, mehr verdaut die Natur[2] nicht. Allein ihr Saft ist soviel wert wie die Kreuzwegstationen den reuelosen Sündern.

[1]Steht auch für das männliche Geschlechtsorgan
[2]Steht auch für das weibliche Geschlechtsorgan

10

HEINRICH ISAAC
Donna di dentro / Dammene un pocho
(Tutti)

Superius

'Donna, di dentro dalla tua casa
son rose, gigli e fiori.
Tuto homo che l'annasa
ne sente gusto al core.
Fortuna d'un gran tempo.
Dammi una rosa.
'Totela, o perla pretiosa.'

Tenor

'Fortuna d'un gran tempo mi se' stata,
O gloriosa donna, mia bella.

Common to all voices

Dammene un pocho di quella
maçacrocha,
e non me ne dar troppa.
[variant:] et dammela ben cotta.

Superius

'Lady, within your house
are roses, lilies, and other flowers.
Every man who smells them
feels their scent in his heart.'
Fortune for a long time.[1]
'Give me a rose.'
'Take it, precious pearl.'

Tenor

'Fortune, for a long time you were,[1]
O glorious lady, my beauty.

Common to all voices

Give me a little of that
mazzacrocca,[2]
but don't give me too much.
and give it to me well baked.

---

[1] A quotation from a famous song.
[2] A long stick-shaped cake or pastry with a knob at the end (probably with an obscene double meaning).

FRANÇAIS

Superius : « Dame, il y a dans ta maison des roses, des lis et d'autres fleurs. Tout homme qui les hume en sent l'odeur dans son cœur. Donne-moi une rose. — Prends-la, perle précieuse. »
Ténor : Fortune, de longtemps tu m'as souri.*
Toutes les voix : Donne-moi un peu de ce long gâteau [*mazzacrocca*] renflé, mais pas trop.

*Citation d'une célèbre chanson de l'époque.

ESPAÑOL

Superius: Señora, el perfume de las flores de tu casa da placer al corazón de los hombres que las huelen.
Tenor: Fortuna de un gran tiempo fuiste, bella mía.[1]
Todas las voces: Dame un poco de esa mazzacrocca[2] bien cocida.

[1]Cita de una famosa canción.
[2]Un pastel o bollo de forma alargada con una protuberancia en un extremo (probablemente con doble sentido).

DEUTSCH

Superius: Herrin, in deinem Haus blühen Rosen. Der Mann, der ihren Duft riecht, fühlt ihn in seinem Herzen.
Tenor: Mein Glück warst du für lange Zeit, o stolze Herrin!
Alle: Reiche mir noch etwas von diesem Mazzacrocca[1], nicht zu viel, aber schön knusprig.

[1]Längliches Gebäck (vermutlich mit obszönem Doppelsinn).

[11] Anonymous, Florentine Carnival Song
Canto di donne maestre di far cacio (Tutti)

Donne no' siàn di Chianti per natione
maestre di far cacio al paragone.

El mestier nostro vuol gran diligenza,
pulitezza, buon occhio e patienza,
fresca la mano et avere avertenza,
pigliare el latte sol d'una ragione.

Bisogna prima aver tutto l'armento
rinchiuse fralle rete o 'n casa drento,
pigliarle una per volta: o che contento
ha quella che è la prima a tal factione!

Presa ch'è l'una, qual sie qui di noi
gli apre le coscie e dalle poppe poi
prieme el latte nel vaso, tal che voi
ben quante noi il faresti in suo stagione.

Come 'l latte è rapreso nel vasello,
bisogna con duo man trarlo di quello,
priemerlo, maneggiarlo et farlo bello,
formarlo et porlo asciutto nel gabbione.

El nostro cacio in sé tutto è perfetto,
non troppo corto, lungo, largo o stretto,
grosso a ragion, ritondo, saldo e netto:
fra 'l terzo e 'l mezo piace a' più persone.

We are ladies born in Chianti,
we have mastered cheese-making at its best.[1]

Our craft requires great diligence,
cleanliness, a good eye, and patience,
a cool hand and paying attention,
taking the milk only in one way.

You must first have the entire herd
shut up in the nets or inside the house,
and take the cows one at a time; Oh what
contentment/has she who is the first of the lot!

Once a cow is taken, any one of us here
opens its legs and then from the teats
squeezes the milk into the pail, just as you
would do to all of us at the right time.

When the milk is curdled in the pail,
you must pull it out with both hands,
squeeze it, knead it, and make it nice,
mould it, and when it is dry put it in the basket.

Our cheese is absolutely perfect,
not too short, long, wide, or narrow;
the right size, round, firm, and clean;
most people like between a third and a half.[2]

[1]Throughout there is a play on *cacio* (cheese) and *cazzo*, the coarse term for the male organ.
[2]The unit in question is the Florentine *braccio* or cubit of 58 cm.

FRANÇAIS

Mesdames, nous sommes les reines du fromage[1]. Notre métier demande de bons yeux, de la patience et des mains fraîches. Quand le lait est caillé dans le vase, il faut l'en retirer à deux mains, le manier, le former et le mettre à sécher. Notre fromage est toujours parfait, ni trop court ni trop long, rond et propre.

[1] Il y a jeu de mots entre *cacio* (fromage) et *cazzo* (appellation vulgaire du pénis).

ESPAÑOL

Señoras, somos de Chianti, maestras en hacer queso.[1] Nuestro trabajo requiere gran diligencia, buen ojo y paciencia. Hay que tener el rebaño encerrado y tomar las vacas una a una. Tomada la primera, se le abren las patas y se aprietan las ubres para que mane la leche. Hay que amasar la leche del balde y darle forma bella. Seca se coloca en una cesta. Nuestro queso es perfecto, de tamaño justo. A la mayoría le gusta entre un tercio y la mitad.[2]

[1] Se juega con las palabras *cacio* (queso) y *cazzo*, término grosero para el órgano masculino.
[2] La unidad es el *braccio* florentino o cúbito de 58 cm.

DEUTSCH

Wir sind Frauen aus Chianti und Meister der Käsebereitung[1]. Unser Handwerk erfordert großes Geschick. Die Kühe werden einzeln gemolken, die Milch wird aus den Zitzen in die Eimer gespritzt. Wenn die Milch geronnen ist, wird sie geknetet, geformt und getrocknet. Dann kommt der Käse ins Körbchen. Unser Käse ist vollkommen, von der richtigen Größe, fest und makellos.

[1] Ital. "cacio" (Käse) (gleichlautend mit "cazzo") ist ein vulgärer Ausdruck für das männliche Geschlechtsorgan.

ITALIANO

Il testo giuoca sulla somiglianza tra 'cacio' e 'cazzo'.

12 GUILLAUME DUFAY
Adieu ces bons vins de Lannoys
(Charles Daniels, Angus Smith, Donald Greig)

Adieu ces bons vins de Lannoys,	Farewell those good wines of the Laonnois,[1]
Adieu dames, adieu borgois,	farewell ladies, farewell burghers,
Adieu celle que tant amoye.	Farewell she whom I so loved.
Adieu toute playsante joye,	Farewell all pleasure and joy.
Adieu tous compagnon galois.	Farewell all boon companions.
Je m'en vois tout arquant des nois,	I depart all weighed down by my load of walnuts,
Car je ne truis feves ne pois,	for I cannot find beans or peas,
Dont bien souvent ou cueur m'ennoye.	at which I feel constant annoyance in my heart.
Adieu ces bons vins de Lannoys,	Farewell those good wines of the Laonnois,
Adieu dames, adieu borgois,	farewell ladies, farewell burghers,
Adieu celle que tant amoye.	farewell she whom I so loved.
De moy serés par plusieurs fois	I shall miss you on many occasions
Regretés par dedans les bois,	within the woods,
Où il n'y a sentier ni voye.	where there is neither foot path nor road.
Puis ne sçaray que faire doye	Then I shall not know what I ought to do,
Se je ne crie à haute vois:	Except to cry aloud:
Adieu ces bons vins de Lannoys,	Farewell those good wines of the Laonnois,
Adieu dames, adieu borgois,	farewell ladies, farewell burghers,
Adieu celle que tant amoye.	farewell she whom I so loved.
Adieu toute playsante joye,	Farewell all pleasure and joy,
Adieu tous compagnon galois.	Farewell all boon companions.

[1] In the Middle Ages the region of Laon was famous for its wines;
production continued till the nineteenth century.

FRANÇAIS

Adieu, bons vins de Laon, dame que j'aime
tant, plaisantes joies, compagnons de plaisirs.
Je m'en vais car je ne trouve ni fèves ni pois.
Je vous regretterai souvent dans les bois,
quand je ne saurai que faire si ce n'est crier :
Adieu, bons vins de Laon…

[1]La région de Laon était célèbre au Moyen Age
pour ses vins. La production a perduré jusqu'au
XIXe siècle.

ESPAÑOL

Adiós vinos de Laon,[1] damas, burgueses, aquella
a quien tanto amé, buenos compañeros. Me voy
cargado de nueces. Me faltaréis tantas veces en
el bosque sin caminos. No sabré qué hacer sino
gritar: adiós vinos de Laon...

[1]En la Edad Media la región de Laon era famosa
por sus vinos. La producción continuó hasta
el s.XIX.

DEUTSCH

Lebt wohl, ihr guten Weine von Laon[1], lebt
wohl, ihr Damen, und die, die ich so liebte, lebt
wohl, Gefährten. Ich gehe gebeugt unter der
Last meines Talents, denn ich habe keinen roten
Heller. Ihr werdet mir fehlen; ich werde mir
keinen Rat mehr wissen, als laut zu rufen:
lebt wohl, ihr guten Weine von Laon.

[1]Die Gegend von Laon war im Mittelalter berühmt
für ihre guten Weine; noch im 19.Jahrhundert
wurde dort Wein angebaut.

ITALIANO

Addio ai buoni vini di Laon[1], addio dame,
cittadini, addio a lei che amavo, al piacere e
alla gioia, ai buoni compagni. Parto con le mie
noci, perchè non trovo fagioli o piselli, il che mi
scoccia. Mi mancherete quando sarò nei boschi,
dove non c'è né sentiero né strada; non saprò
cos'altro fare se non gridare 'addio'!

[1]Regione conosciuta per la produzione del vino nel
medioevo; la produzione continua fino al secolo 19.

13 GILLES BINCHOIS
Je ne vis onques la pareille
(Robert Harre-Jones, Charles Daniels, Donald Greig)

Je ne vis onques la pareille
De vous, ma gracieuse dame;
Car vo beaulté est par mon ame
Sur toutes aultres nonpareille.

En vois voiant je m'esmerveille,
Et dis: qu'est ceci, nostre Dame?
Je ne vis onques la pareille
De vous, ma gracieuse dame;

Vostre tres grant doulceur resveille
Mon esprit, et mon oeil entame
Mon cuer, dont puis dire sans blame,
Puis qu'a vous servir m'apareille,

Je ne vis onques la pareille
De vous, ma gracieuse dame;
Car vo beaulté est par mon ame
Sur toutes aultres nonpareille.

I never saw a woman like you,
my gracious lady;
For your beauty is, by my soul,
matchless above all others.

Looking at you I marvel,
And say, what is this, our Lady?
I never saw a woman like you,
my gracious lady;

Your great sweetness awakens
my spirit, and my eye reads deep in
my heart, wherefore I may say without censure,
since I prepare myself to serve you:

I never saw a woman like you,
my gracious lady;
For your beauty is, by my soul,
unmatched above all others.

FRANÇAIS

Jamais je ne vis de beauté pareille à la vôtre, gracieuse dame. Je m'émerveille et dis : qu'est ceci, notre Dame ? Votre grande douceur réveille mon esprit, et mon œil lit dans mon cœur : puisque je m'apprête à vous servir, je puis dire que jamais je ne vis de beauté pareille…

ESPAÑOL

A nadie conozco, mi graciosa dama, de belleza como la vuestra. Me maravilla miraros. Vuestra dulzura despierta mi alma y sólo quiero serviros. A nadie conozco, mi graciosa dama, de belleza como la vuestra.

DEUTSCH

Nie habe ich eine gesehen wie Euch, bezaubernde Herrin, denn Eure Schönheit ist unvergleichlich. Ich bin entzückt von Eurem Anblick, eure Anmut erquickt mein Gemüt; so kann ich sagen, da ich mich anschicke, Euch zu dienen: nie habe ich eine gesehen wie Euch.

ITALIANO

Non ho mai visto donna come voi, gentile signora, bella più di ogni altra. Vi guardo e mi chiedo—è costei Madonna? La vostra dolcezza sveglia lo spirito, e l'occhio penetra fino al cuore, e dico senza riguardo, dal momento che mi preparo a servirvi: non ho mai visto donna come voi, gentile signora, bella più di ogni altra.

LOYSET COMPÈRE
Sile fragor
(Tutti)

Sile fragor ac rerum tumultus	Be silent, noise and bustle of the world;
fuge pavor qui pectore raucus anhelas.	fly, fear, that breathes hoarsely in the breast.
Psallere nos sine et nostros aequare modos.	Allow us to perform our music and keep in tune;
Urget amor Musae	The love of the muse spurs us on,
opprimens iurgia irae	suppressing the brawls of wrath,
cum ecclesia resonat dulcore carminis nostri	when the church echoes to the sweetness of our song
et voces solidae audientium aures demulcent.	and our firm voices charm the listeners' ears.
Suscipe, deitatis mater,	Receive, Mother of the Godhead,
vocum praecordia nostra.	our hearts, contained in our voices,
et nato refunde vota	and pour forth to thy Son in turn the prayers
quae psallimus omnes.	that we all sing.
Nunc fontem adire decet	Now it is meet to approach the fountain
quo Bacchus insedet ipse	on which Bacchus himself is enthroned,
et discedat lympha	and let water depart
Liberi* dum carpimus rivos. Amen.	while we draw Liber's [= Bacchus'] streams. Amen.
Amen.	Amen.

*The manuscript has *liberos* (the free streams), corrected by Dr. Jeffrey Dean.

FRANÇAIS

Silence, tumulte du monde, laisse-nous chanter et comparer nos mélodies. L'amour de la muse nous presse, l'église résonne de nos chants suaves et nos voix charment les auditeurs. Soutiens nos cœurs, mère de la divinité. Il convient à présent d'aller vers la fontaine où trône Bacchus lui-même : que l'eau fasse place aux ruisseaux de vin.

ESPAÑOL

Calla, fragor del mundo. Vuela, miedo que anida en el pecho. Déjanos tocar en nuestros modos. El amor de la musa nos espolea cuando deleitamos a los oyentes. Recibe, madre de la divinidad, nuestros corazones y lleva a tu hijo nuestros salmos. Es el momento de ir a la fuente de Baco y libar de sus corrientes.[1] Amén.

[1]En el manuscrito figura *liberos* (las corrientes libres), corregido por el Dr Jeffrey Dean.

DEUTSCH

Schweig, Getöse der Welt, laß uns musizieren. Die Liebe zur Muse besänftigt den Zorn, wenn die Kirche widerhallt von unserm Gesang. Nimm an, Mutter der Gottheit, unsere Herzen und überbringe deinem Sohn die Gebete, die wir singen. Zum Brunnen des Bacchus zu treten ziemt es sich jetzt, daß wir uns laben an seinen Strömen. Amen.

ITALIANO

Si calmi il fracasso mondano, fugga la paura dal petto. Lasciateci fare la nostra musica senza stonare; l'amore per la musa ci incita scacciando l'ira; riempiamo la chiesa col canto e le nostre voci sicure lusingano gli ascoltatori. Ricevi, Madre di Dio, i nostri cuori, e porta a tuo Figlio queste preghiere cantate. Ci avviciniamo alla fontana di Bacco; l'acqua esce mentre traiamo i rivoli del dio.

15 Anonymous
La plus grant chière
(Robert Harre-Jones, Angus Smith, Donald Greig)

La plus grant chiere de jamais	The grandest banquet ever
Ont fait à Cambrai la cite	was held in the city of Cambrai
Morton et Hayne, en verité,	by Morton[1] and Hayne[2]; indeed
On ne vous pourroit dire mais.	there is nothing more to say.
S'ont esté servis de beaux mais	They were served with fine dishes
Tout part tout où ilz ont esté.	absolutely everywhere they went.
La plus grant chiere de jamais . . .	The grandest banquet ever . . .
Encores vous jure et prometz,	Moreover, I swear and promise you,
Sur bas instrumens à planté	on low instruments in plenty
Ont joué et si fort chanté	they played and sang so loud
Qu'on les a ouÿ pres de Mais.	they could be heard around Metz.
La plus grant chiere de jamais . . .	The grandest banquet ever . . .

[1]Robert Morton (c.1430–c.1497), English composer at Burgundian court, ?later bishop of Worcester.
[2]Hayne van Ghizeghem (c.1445–before 1497), Flemish composer at Burgundian and probably French courts.

FRANÇAIS

Jamais Morton* et Hayne* ne firent meilleure chère qu'à Cambrai, en vérité. De beaux mets leur ont été servis partout où ils sont allés. Je vous jure aussi qu'ils ont si fort joué et chanté qu'on les a entendus jusqu'à Metz.

*L'Anglais Robert Morton (v. 1430–v. 1497) et le Flamand Hayne van Ghizeghem (v. 1445– avt 1497), compositeurs de la cour de Bourgogne.

DEUTSCH

Das größte Gelage aller Zeiten hielten in Cambrai Morton[1] und Hayne[2]. Feinste Speisen wurden ihnen allenthalben gereicht. Sie spielten, glaubt mir, auf Instrumenten von lieblichem Klang und sangen so laut, daß man sie bis Metz hören konnte.

[1] Robert Morton (um 1430–um 1497), englischer Komponist am burgundischen Hof, möglicherweise später Bischof von Worcester.
[2] Hayne van Ghizeghem (um 1445–vor 1497), flämischer Komponist am burgundischen und wahrscheinlich auch am französischen Hof.

ESPAÑOL

En Cambrai, Morton[1] y Hayne[2] hicieron una gran fiesta. Se les sirvieron platos por doquier. En Cambrai... Tocaron y cantaron tan fuerte que podía oírse en Metz. En Cambrai...

[1] Robert Morton (c.1430–c.1497), compositor inglés en la corte de Borgoña, ségun algunas fuentes fue también obispo de Worcester.
[2] Hayne van Ghizeghem (c.1445–antes de 1497), compositor flamenco en las cortes de Borgoña y, tal vez, Francia.

ITALIANO

La più grande festa mai offerta fu quella di Morton[1] e Hayne[2] a Cambrai—tanto che non c'è niente altro da dire. Furono serviti piatti deliziosi in ogni luogo, e per di più vi giuro che suonarono e cantarono su tanti strumenti dolci con tanta forza che si sentirono fino a Metz.

[1] Robert Morton (c.1430-c.1497), compositore inglese alla corte di Borgogna, e forse anche vescovo di Worcester.
[2] Hayne van Ghizeghem (c.1445-ante 1497), compositore fiammingo alla corte di Borgogna e forse anche alla corte francese.

16 Anonymous

La tricotea

(Charles Daniels, Angus Smith, Donald Greig)

This text is a sort of mock-Spanish gibberish. The first two lines are based on a French chanson text: *La triquotée s'est par matin levée, / S'a pris sa harpe, au bois s'en est allée* (The loose woman rose in the morning, took her harp, and went off to the wood) but turn them into Spanish or nearly Spanish words of roughly similar sound: *La tricotea, Samartín la vea, / Ábres(e) un poc al agua y señalea* (The *tricotea*, let St Martin see it, Opens a little to the water and gives a signal). 'Tricotea' has no meaning in Spanish. Thereafter it continues in broken Spanish, broken Italian, and broken Portuguese: 'La bota' may be 'the boat' or 'the wineskin', 'sembra' may be broken Spanish for 'sows' (correctly 'siembra') or Italian 'seems', but 'tuleta' means nothing in either language. I have translated those phrases that make some sort of sense (mostly to do with food and drink) and rendered the rest with English nonsense that sounds vaguely like the original (marked with an asterisk). – L. H.-S.

La tricotea, Samartín la vea,	The trick or treat, St. Martin's Day can have it;*
abres un poc al agua y señalea.	Adversary, poke an ague and send 'All clear'*
La bota sembra tuleta,	The boat's assembled too late*
la señal de un chapiré.	the arsenal of a chap at bay*
Ge que te gus per mundo spesa	Hey, I enjoy you all over the world,
la botilla plena.	full bottle,
Dama qui maina,	Leading lady,
cerrali la vena.	merrily you labour.*
Orli cerli trum madama	Now then shut tight, madam,
cerlicer cerrarli ben	shut them, shut them, shut them well
votra a mi contrari ben.	your interest opposed to mine.
Niquiniquidón formagi dón,	Knick-knack paddywhack, give cheeses,
formagi dón.	give cheeses.
Yo soy monarquea de grande nobrea.	I am a monarch of great nobility
Dama por amor,	lady for love's sake,
dama bel se mea;	the fair lady's pissing herself;
dama yo la vea.	the lady, may I see her.

FRANÇAIS

Le début de la chanson reprend les deux premiers vers de la chanson française « La Triquotée » auxquels elle donne une consonance espagnole. Dans la suite du texte, le locuteur rend hommage au vin, s'adresse à une dame et se dit monarque de grande noblesse. La joyeuse incohérence des propos veut peut-être évoquer les divagations d'un ivrogne.

ESPAÑOL

Este texto es una especie de galimatías en español burlesco. Las dos primeras líneas están basadas en una canción francesa: *La disoluta se levantó por la mañana, / tomó su arpa y salió al bosque,* pero al tomar palabras de sonido similar en español o semi-español: *La tricotea, Samartín la vea, / Ábres(e) un poc al agua y señalea.* 'Tricotea' no significa nada. Y así prosigue en medio español, medio italiano, medio portugués: 'La bota' puede ser 'la barca' o 'la piel para el vino', 'sembra' puede ser 'siembra' o el italiano 'parece', pero 'tuleta' no existe en ninguna de estas lenguas.

DEUTSCH

Dieser Text ist ein Kauderwelsch aus mehreren Sprachen. Die ersten beiden Zeilen gehen auf eine französische Chanson zurück, die rein dem Klang nach in ein Nonsens-Spanisch übertragen wurde, dann geht es weiter in gebrochenem Spanisch, Italienisch und Portugiesisch. Eine Aussage enthält der Text nicht, es handelt sich um reine Klangspielereien.

ITALIANO

Questo testo è una specie di filastrocca assurda in finto spagnolo. I primi due versi prendono lo spunto da una canzone francese: *La puttana si alzò un mattino, / prese l'arpa, e si avviò verso il bosco,* dell'originale mantengono il suono, però modificando le parole per imitare più o meno lo spagnolo: *La tricotea, come vede San Martino, Apre verso l'acqua e fa un segnale.* 'Tricotea' non ha significato alcuno in spagnolo. Da questo punto, i versi continuano imitando maccheronicamente lo spagnolo, l'italiano, e il portoghese: 'la bota' può significare 'barca' o 'borraccia'; 'sembra' potrebbe essere un tentativo allo spagnolo 'scrofa' (siembra), o all'italiano 'sembra'; ma 'tuleta' non si trova in nessuna di queste lingue.

17 JUAN PONCE
Ave color vini clari
(Tutti)

Ave color vini clari	Hail, colour of clear wine,
Ave sapor sine pari	Hail, taste without peer.
Tua nos inebriari	Deign to make us drunk
Digneris potencia.	by thy power
O quam felix creatura	O how blessed a creature.
Quam produxit vitis pura	brought forth by the pure vine,
Omnis mensa sit secura	May every table be free of care
In tua presencia.	in thy presence.
O quam placens in colore,	O how pleasing in colour,
O quam fragrans in odore,	O how fragrant a bouquet,
O quam sapidum in ore,	O how savourous in the mouth,
Dulce linguis vinculum!	sweet shackle for tongues!
Felix venter quem intrabis,	Happy the belly thou shalt enter,
Felix guttur quod rigabis,	Happy the throat that thou shalt moisten,
O felix os quod lavabis,	O happy the mouth that thou shalt rinse,
O beata labia!	O blessed lips!
Ergo vinum collaudemus,	Therefore let us praise wine together,
potatores exaltemus;	and exalt drinkers;
Non potantes confundemus	on non-drinkers we shall bring confusion
In eterna secula. Amen.	unto all eternity. Amen.

FRANÇAIS

Ave, couleur du vin clair, saveur sans pareille, veuille nous enivrer. Qu'elle soit sans crainte la table où il y a du vin pur. Heureux le ventre qui t'absorbe, heureux le gosier que tu mouilles, heureuse la bouche que tu laves. Louons le vin, exaltons les buveurs. Confondons les non-buveurs pour l'éternité. Amen.

ESPAÑOL

Ave, vinos de color claro y sabor sin igual. Vuestra potencia nos embriaga. Toda mesa está segura con vuestra presencia. ¡Qué agradables color, olor y sabor! Felices sean el vientre en que entráis y la boca que laváis. Alabemos el vino y quienes no beben caigan en la confusión por siempre jamás. Amén.

DEUTSCH

Heil dir, Farbe des Weins, mache uns trunken. Von jedem Tisch, den du zierst, sei die Sorge verbannt. Oh, wie wunderbar ist dein Bouquet, wie köstlich ist dein Geschmack. Glücklich die Kehle, die du benetzt! Laßt uns den Wein rühmen und die Trinker preisen, den Nichttrinkern werden wir ewig ein Ärgernis sein. Amen.

ITALIANO

Ave, colore e sapore del vino, inebriaci col tuo potere. Benedetta sia la creatura prodotta dal vino puro; alla tua presenza sia spensierata ogni tavola. Piacevoli il colore e il profumo, delizioso il sapore che lega la lingua! Felice la pancia che riempi, la gola che bagni, la bocca che risciacqui; benedette labbra! Lodiamo il vino, esaltiamo i bevitori; portiamo confusione eterna agli astemi. Amen.

JUAN DEL ENCINA
Oy comamos y bebamos
(Tutti)

Oy comamos y bebamos,	Today let us eat and drink,
y cantemos y holguemos,	and sing and be merry,
que mañana ayunaremos.	for tomorrow we shall fast.
Por onrra de Sant Antruejo	For the honour of St. Carnival,
parémonos oy bien anchos,	let's fatten ourselves well today,
embutamos estos panchos,	let's fill up these paunches,
rrecalquemos el pellejo,	let's cram our hide,
que costumbre es de conçejo	for it is a wise custom
que todos oy nos hartemos,	that we all stuff ourselves today,
que mañana ayunaremos.	for tomorrow we shall fast.
Honrremos a tan buen santo,	Let us honour so good a saint,
porque en hambre nos acorra;	that he may help us in hunger;
comamos a calcaporra,	let us eat and bloat ourselves
que mañana ay gran quebranto.	for tomorrow there'll be great exhaustion.
Comamos, bebamos tanto,	Let us eat and drink
hasta que nos rrebentemos,	until we absolutely burst,
que mañana ayunaremos.	for tomorrow we shall fast.
Beve, Bras; más tú, Beneyto,	Drink, Braz; all the more, Benedict,
beva Pidruelo y Llorente;	Let Pidruelo and Llorente drink;
beve tú primeramente,	you drink first of all,
quitarnos has deste preito.	let's quit arguing.
En beber bien me deleyto;	I take great delight in drinking;
dacá, dacá, beberemos,	come, pour, we shall drink,
que mañana ayunaremos.	for tomorrow we shall fast.

Tomemos oy gasajado,
que mañana vien la muerte;
bebamos, comamos huerte;
vámonos para el ganado.
No perderemos bocado,
que comiendo nos iremos,
que mañana ayunaremos.

FRANÇAIS
Mangeons et buvons, chantons et amusons-
nous, car demain nous jeûnerons. Remplissons-
nous la panse, mangeons et buvons à éclater.
Bois en premier, cela mettra fin à cette querelle.
Je me délecte à boire. Prenons du plaisir aujour-
d'hui, car demain vient la mort. Mangeons et
n'en perdons pas une bouchée, car demain nous
jeûnerons.

Let us take our pleasure today,
for death will come tomorrow;
let us drink and eat with vigour;
let us go off to the herd.
We shall not waste a morsel,
but shall eat as we go.
for tomorrow we shall fast.

DEUTSCH
Laßt uns heute essen und trinken, singen
und lachen, denn morgen werden wir fasten.
Wir wollen uns den Wanst vollschlagen, dem
heiligen Carneval zu Ehren, damit er uns
beisteht in Zeiten des Hungers. Kommt, laßt
uns trinken, laßt uns heute vergnügt sein,
denn morgen schon kommt der Tod. Es soll
kein Bissen vergeudet sein, denn morgen
werden wir fasten.

ITALIANO
Oggi mangiamo e beviamo e cantiamo perchè
domani digiuneremo. Facciamo una bella
abbuffata per Carnevale; onoriamo questo santo
benevolo, che ci aiuti quando avremo fame—
mangiamo e beviamo fino a scoppiare. Bevete,
Braz, Benedetto, Pidruelo e Llorente; bere mi
piace molto. Divertiamoci oggi, perchè domani
moriremo; andiamo alle mandrie, mangiando e
bevendo di strada, perchè domani digiuneremo.

19 Anonymous
Quem tem farelos
(Robert Harre-Jones, Angus Smith, Donald Greig)

'Quem tem farelos, quem tem farelos
de trigo não de centeio?
Venda-me, venda-me este saco cheio.

Passe senhora a farinha
com tempo que estou de pressa.'
'Aqui estou nesta travessa
falando com a vizinha.'
'Tire os farelos asinha,
de trigo não de centeio.
Venda-me, venda-me este saco cheio.'

'Farelos tenho, mas não'
acabei de peneirar.'
'A como mos há-de dar?'
'A vintém não tem razão,
a dezanove mos dão.'
'Mas a dezassete e meio,
Venda-me, venda-me este saco cheio.

Acabe de peneirar
a farinha do celeiro,
quando tomar o dinheiro
que trago para lhe dar;
que do meu me há-de custar
e não do suor alheio.
Venda-me, venda-me este saco cheio.

'Who has any bran, who has any bran
of wheat, not of rye?
Sell me some, sell me enough to fill this sack.

Sift the flour quickly,
madam, for I'm in a hurry.'
'Here I am in the alley
having a chat with my neighbour.'
'Get the bran out quickly,
of wheat, not of rye.
Sell me some, sell me enough to fill this sack.'

I have some bran, but I haven't
finished sifting it.'
'How much will you sell it me for?'
'For twenty réis is no good,
they give it to me for nineteen.'
'But for seventeen and a half,
Sell me some, sell me enough to fill this sack.

Finish sifting
the granary flour
when you take the money
I am bringing you;
for it cost me
my own sweat and no one else's.
Sell me some, sell me enough to fill this sack.'

FRANÇAIS

« Qui a de la farine ? J'en veux plein ce sac, et
vite, je suis pressé. – Je suis là, dans l'allée. J'ai
de la farine, mais je n'ai pas fini de la cribler. –
Combien la vendez-vous ? – Vingt ce n'est pas
assez, je l'ai achetée dix-neuf. – Remplissez ce
sac pour dix-sept et demi et finissez de la
cribler. »

DEUTSCH

"Wer hat Kleie vom Weizen? Verkauft mir
genug, diesen Sack hier zu füllen. Siebt schnell
das Mehl, meine Dame, ich bin in Eile. – Ich
habe Kleie, aber ich bin noch nicht fertig mit
Sieben. – Was soll es kosten? – Ich bekomme
es für neunzehn. – Verkauft es mir für siebzehn-
einhalb, denn es kostet mich meinen Schweiß
uns sonst keinen."

ESPAÑOL

"¿Quién tiene salvado de trigo? Véndame este
saco lleno, rápido, que tengo prisa. – Salvado
tengo pero no lo terminé de tamizar. – Termine,
que le he de dar el dinero que me ha costado mi
propio sudor. Véndame este saco lleno."

ITALIANO

'Chi ha della crusca non di segale ma di grano?
Vendetemene da riempire questo sacco, che
ho fretta.' – 'Io ne ho, ma ancora devo
setacciarla; sono in strada che parlo con la
vicina.' – 'Quanto costa? Venti réis sono troppi:
facciamo diciannove. Ma per diciassette e mezzo
riempite questo sacco. Fate presto, ecco i soldi;
pago io solo, e nessun'altro.'

Von Eyren
(Tutti)

Ein seltzam newe abenthewr	A strange new adventure
bringen wir mit vns herfür;	we have come here to tell;
ist vor nie hier gewesen,	It has never happened here before,
ein seltzam war,	a strange tale,
nun sehen dar,	now see here,
ist weiß und heissen Eyer.	it is white and they are called eggs.
Das wir die eyer her hand bracht	That we have brought the eggs here
hat freytag und der sambstag gmacht.	is due to Friday and Saturday.
Die eyer muß man teglich han,	Eggs must be eaten every day,
teglich han;	eaten every day;
dem gsunden und dem krancken	the healthy man and the sick
und aderlassern junckern	and bloodletters' boys
wölln wir allsam mit eyern gwern.	we have nourishing eggs for them all.
So hand wir da henneneyr,	So we have hens' eggs,
Genßeyr, enteneyr,	goose eggs, ducks' eggs,
krebseyr, daubeneyr,	crabs' eggs, pigeons' eggs,
nesteyr, hirteneyr,	nest eggs, herdsmen's eggs,
gaucheyr, pfaweneyr,	cuckoos' eggs, peacocks' eggs,
haseneyr, strausseneyr,	hares' eggs, ostrich eggs,
kelbereyr, lange eyr,	calves' eggs, long eggs,
und noch ein groß par eyer,	and a big pair of eggs besides
die hat da unser meyer,	belonging to our farmer,
die hand ir nit gesehen?	haven't you seen them?
So manchen schrey, so manches ey,	As many a squawk, so many an egg
thund unser hennen legen;	do our hens lay;
Und das ist war, ein ey ist weiß,	and this much is true, an egg is white,
Und das ist war, ein ey ist weiß.	and this much is true, an egg is white.

continued on page 68

FRANÇAIS

Mangez des œufs, tout le monde doit en manger, les bien-portants comme les malades. Nous avons des œufs de poule, d'oie, de cane, de pigeon, de coucou, de hase, d'autruche. Et aussi la grosse paire d'œufs de notre fermier, l'avez-vous vue ? Les œufs, nous les mangeons à la coque, frits, durs, farcis ou avec du sain-doux et du sel. Et avec l'œuf, un gorgeon.

ESPAÑOL

Una nueva aventura os venimos a contar. Son blancos y se llaman huevos. Hay que comerlos cada día. Tenemos nutritivos huevos de todas clases para sanos, enfermos y jóvenes. Por cada graznido ponen nuestras gallinas un huevo. Y es verdad que son blancos. Me gusta comer huevos por la mañana, preparados de muchas formas. Y para quien lo merece, sobre un huevo una bebida. Y esto es todo sobre los huevos.

DEUTSCH

gwern = zugute kommen lassen
gaucheyr = Kuckuckseier / ancken = Butter
gsternet = gestürzt / gellerisch = kräftig

ITALIANO

Raccontiamo una strana avventura, una storia nuova—guardate, sono bianche e si chiamano 'uova'. Ve le portiamo perchè è Venerdì e Sabato; le uova si mangiano tutti i giorni, ne abbiamo per sani e per malati, e per i garzoni dei medici. Abbiamo uova di gallina, oca, anatra; di granchio, di piccione, di nido, di pastore; di cucù, pavone, lepre, struzzo, e vitello; uova lunghe, e persino due grosse uova del nostro fattore—non le avete viste? Mi piace mangiar uova al mattino, con tanto burro. Si fanno bollite, fritte, al forno, brillanti, ripiene, al lardo, ma non senza sale. Al mattino si beve il brodo di uova, con dopo un bicchierino. Rompete quelle uova—con una bella botta!

Von Eyren *continued from page 66*

Eyer, eyer
eß ich gern am morgen frü,
der mirs in ein pfenlin schlieg
vil ancken dran.
Auß den eyern, mit den eyern
machen wir gsotten eyr,
braten eyr, bachen eyr,
gsternet eyr, gfüllte eyr
darzu ein ey im schmaltz,
die ißt man nit on salz.
Und auch ein eyerbrü,
eß wir am morgen frü,
ja wers verdient hat
Und auff ein ey ein trunck,
ein gellerischen schwunk
On keck, Hennengeck,
wags ey am kopf entzwey!
noch baß! nun hab du das!
Und das ist von der eyer wegen.

Eggs, eggs,
I like eating them in the mornings,
if someone has put in a pan for me
a lot of butter on top.
From eggs, with eggs
we make boiled eggs,
fried eggs, baked eggs,
spangled* eggs, stuffed eggs,
and an egg in lard as well,
one doesn't eat them without salt.
and an egg broth too
we eat of a morning,
whoever has if anyone has deserved it
and on top of an egg a drink,
a hearty blow
without rashness, hen's squawk,
whack the egg on its head in two!
Harder! Now take that!
And that's all down to eggs!

*upside-down eggs

21 LUDWIG SENFL
Von edler Art
(Tutti)

Von edler Art
spieb ich in Bart
ohn alls Gefähr.
Trüeg ich so schwer
von starkem Wein,
füert man mich heim
in Sessel bald,
drin ich erkalt
und spieb ein Bahn
es möcht einr han
ein Schifflein gfüert
ganz unverrüert.

In noble wise
I spew into my beard
without a thought.
However much I were
weighed down/by strong wine,
I am taken home
soon enough in a chair,
in which I cool down
and spew a passageway,
you could have taken
a boat along it
without any shaking.

Wie ich ihm tue,
Schaffst du kein Rueh',
Spat und auch frue
man singt dir zue,
mein lieber Wein.
Du schleichst hinein
eh ich wird gwahr
der großen Schar
von Gläsern viel.
Zue diesem Spiel
gehört nur Spein,
wes glauben will.

Whatever I do,
you never rest,
Late and early
you are sung to,
my darling wine.
You creep in
before I am aware
of the great troop
of many glasses.
For this game
spewing alone will do,
belive you me!

Seit du der bist,
gen dem ich List
kein Stund nit brauch,
möcht nur in Bauch
ganz Kübel voll.
Und sollt ich toll
werden davon,
so hüeb ich an
und spieb mit Fleiß
in solcher Weis,
als hätt ich des
den höchsten Preis.

Since you are the one
against whom I
never use cunning,
though you should enter my belly
in whole bucketfuls.
And even if I should
go mad from it,
I should set to
and spew and spew
just as if
that were the way
to the highest glory.

FRANÇAIS

Quand je suis saoul, on me ramène chez moi
en fauteuil, et là, je prends froid et je vomis.
Il vaudrait mieux un petit bateau. Cher vin, tu
fais effet avant que j'aie pu compter les verres.
À ce jeu-là, il convient de vomir, croyez-moi.
Et si cela devait me rendre fou, je continuerais
à boire et à vomir avec zèle.

DEUTSCH

spieb = ich speite
ohn alls Gefähr = ohne viel Umstände

ESPAÑOL

Con nobleza vomito en mi barba sin pensar.
He bebido tanto que me llevan a casa sobre
una silla en la que vuelvo a vomitar. Querido
vino, haga lo que haga nunca descansas. Entras
sin que me aperciba del tropel de vasos. Contra
ti nunca uso astucias, aunque llenas mi vientre
como un cubo. Y aunque enloquezca, vomitaré y
vomitaré como si ése fuera el camino a la gloria.

ITALIANO

Nobilmente vomito nella barba senza rimpianti.
Ben pieno di vino, vado a casa in portantina
rinfrescandomi, e vomito per strada tanto da
andarci in barca. Tu non riposi mai: ti canto
mattina e sera, caro vino mio. Entri furtiva-
mente: neanche mi accorgo delle legioni di
bicchieri. Non mi difendo, e anche se dovessi
impazzire vomito come se fosse cosa gloriosa.

22 Anonymous
Trinkt und singt
(Tutti)

Trinkt und singt und springt herum,
diri, diri, diri dum!
Welcher Cato wollt uns wehren,
fröhlich sein in allen Ehren?

Drink and sing and leap about,
diri, diri, diri dum!
What Cato* would prevent us
from being honourably merry?

Trinkt und singt . . .
Schwenket aus die großen Krausen,
keiner wöll ihm lassen grausen.

Drink and sing . . .
Bottoms up with the great tankards,
let no one take offence.

Trinkt und singt . . .
Keiner tu vom andern weichen,
laßt die Gläslein umherschleichen,

Drink and sing . . .
Let no one lag behind his neighbour,
let the glasses slide around,

Trinkt und singt . . .
Guter Wein, der labt das Herze,
frisch das Blut und legt den Schmerzen.

Drink and sing . . .
Good wine cleanses the heart,
quickens the blood and allays sorrows.

Trinkt und singt . . .
Rucket immer baß zusammen,
ghabt euch wohl in Gottes Namen,

Drink and sing . . .
Draw together, closer and closer
enjoy yourselves in God's name,

Trinkt und singt . . .
Dieser Wirt, der will uns borgen
von nun an bis auf den Morgen.

Drink and sing . . .
This host is willing to lend us money
from now until the morning.
English translations by Leofranc Holford-Strevens

*Probably Cato the Censor, Roman statesman, 234 BC–149 BC

FRANÇAIS

Buvez, chantez et dansez ! Qui nous empêchera d'être joyeux ? Que les verres circulent. Le bon vin ranime le cœur, rafraîchit le sang et apaise les douleurs. Restez ensemble et amusez-vous sans remords. L'aubergiste nous fait crédit jusqu'au matin.

Traduit par Jacqueline Letteron

ESPAÑOL

Bebe y danza y salta. ¿Qué Catón nos impide ser felices? Voltead las gorgueras y que nadie se ofenda. Que nadie quede atrás. El buen vino limpia el corazón y alivia el dolor. Uníos y disfrutad en nombre de Dios. El tabernero nos fía hasta la mañana.

Interpretaciones por Anna Mateo

DEUTSCH

Cato = römischer Zensor

Übersetzungen von Heidi Fritz

ITALIANO

Bevete, cantate, e saltate, diri diri diri dum! Quale Catone ci impedirebbe di essere onestamente allegri? Alzate il gomito, non offendetevi, non fatevi sorpassare dal vicino, muovete quei bicchieri, il buon vino purifica il cuore, fa scorrere il sangue, cura il dolore. Avvicinatevi l'un l'altro, divertitevi, per Dio, che l'oste ci fa credito fino al mattino.

Tradotto da Massimo Ossi

Michael Putland

(from left to right) Donald Greig *baritone*, Robert Harre-Jones *countertenor*, Angus Smith *tenor*, Charles Daniels *tenor*.

THE ORLANDO CONSORT

Robert Harre-Jones *countertenor* Charles Daniels *tenor*
Angus Smith *tenor* Donald Greig *baritone*

Formed by the Early Music Centre of Great Britain for a 1988 national tour, the ORLANDO CONSORT rapidly became one of the most reputed and innovative exponents of vocal repertoire of the eleventh to fourteenth centuries. All four members of the Consort are established soloists prized for their experience with such groups as the Tallis Scholars, the Gabrieli Consort, and the Taverner Consort. In collaboration with leading experts in Medieval and Renaissance music, the ORLANDO CONSORT has premiered fascinating repertoire unheard in modern times and has set new standards of performance, particularly in matters of pronunciation and tuning. Research into the extraordinary techniques of twelfth-century Aquitanian polyphony earned the Consort the **1996 Noah Greenberg Award** from the American Musicological Society.

The group has garnered numerous distinctions, including the **1996 Gramophone Award for Early Music** and an Edison Award nomination, and has been short-listed 5 times for further Gramophone Awards. The Consort now records exclusively for Harmonia Mundi USA.

The ORLANDO CONSORT — a frequent guest at International festivals in Europe and North America — tours extensively in the United States and Japan, and has appeared in Greece, Russia, and South America, with future visits planned to Holland, Italy, Spain and the Czech Republic. In April 2000, the Consort performed the inaugural concert at the National Centre for Early Music in York.

The work of the ORLANDO CONSORT extends beyond early music and has attracted considerable attention in recent years for imaginative programming of contemporary music. Forthcoming projects include collaborations with the jazz quartet Perfect Houseplants and with The Dufay Collective.

For more information on the ORLANDO CONSORT,
please visit www.orlandoconsort.com

L'ORLANDO CONSORT

Robert Harre-Jones *countertenor* Charles Daniels *tenor*
Angus Smith *tenor* Donald Greig *baritone*

Formé par l'Early Music Centre de Grande-Bretagne en vue d'une tournée nationale en 1988, l'ORLANDO CONSORT est rapidement devenu l'un des interprètes les plus réputés et les plus novateurs du répertoire vocal né entre le XIe et le XIVe siècle. Ses quatre membres sont des solistes reconnus, riches de leur expérience au sein de groupes comme les Tallis Scholars, le Gabrieli Consort et le Taverner Consort. Avec la collaboration des meilleurs experts de la musique du Moyen Âge et de la Renaissance, l'ORLANDO CONSORT a tiré de l'oubli un répertoire fascinant et a fixé de nouvelles normes d'interprétation, particulièrement en matière de prononciation et d'accord. Ses recherches sur l'extraordinaire polyphonie aquitaine du XIIe siècle lui ont valu le Noah Greenberg Award, que l'American Musicological Society lui a décerné en 1996.

L'ensemble a glané de nombreuses distinctions, dont le Gramophone Award for Early Music en 1996 et une nomination à l'Edison Award, et il a été sélectionné cinq fois pour des Gramophone Awards. Aujourd'hui, le Consort enregistre exclusivement pour **harmonia mundi usa**.

Régulièrement invité dans les festivals internationaux d'Europe et d'Amérique du Nord, l'ORLANDO CONSORT fait de fréquentes tournées aux États-Unis et au Japon. Il s'est également produit en Grèce, en Russie, en Amérique du Sud, et donnera des concerts aux Pays-Bas, en Italie, en Espagne et en République tchèque. En avril 2000, le Consort a donné le concert inaugural du National Centre for Early Music de York.

Étendant son champ d'activité au-delà de la musique ancienne, l'ORLANDO CONSORT a suscité une vive attention au cours de ces dernières années par l'inventivité de ses programmes de musique contemporaine. Il a entre autres projets ceux de collaborer avec le quartette de jazz Perfect Houseplants et avec le Dufay Collective.

**Pour plus d'informations sur l'ORLANDO CONSORT,
rendez-vous sur le www.orlandoconsort.com**

s fa lauoreri de latte

neueue si fa

Luochi freschi doue fu lauoreri de latte

latte micte si fa

The Cooks

Best known for riding around in a motorbike sidecar and as a TV co-host of **Two Fat Ladies** with Jennifer Patterson, **CLARISSA DICKSON WRIGHT** has a cookery bookshop at the Grassmarket in Edinburgh, a café at Lennoxlove House, family house of the Dukes of Hamilton, and is rector of Aberdeen University, Scotland.

ROZ DENNY is a London-based food writer and cookbook author. Her work includes a wide range of subjects, from ethnic food, to interpreting the recipes of Michelin 3-star chef Gordon Ramsay, to recreating Tudor recipes for the Royal kitchens at Hampton Court. Her latest book, **Modern German Cooking**, is due out later this year from Simon & Schuster.

JEAN-CHRISTOPHE NOVELLI, began his career as a baker at 14, becoming head private chef to the Rothschild family before the age of 20. On his arrival in England he worked for various country house hotels and as chef-manager of Keith Floyd's pub and restaurant, winning awards for "Face of the Future" as well as "Country Restaurant of the Year" three times. After opening several restaurants in London and earning numerous Michelin stars, Jean-Christophe Novelli is now back behind the stoves of the highly successful **Maison Novelli**, Clerkenwell Green, in London where he remains passionate about restaurants and his cooking.

FOOD, WINE & SONG

In 1987 **RUTH ROGERS** and **ROSE GRAY** founded the **River Cafe** in London. Since opening the restaurant, Ruth and Rose have produced three best-selling River Cafe cookbooks. Both chefs have spent much time living and cooking in Italy. Their adapted recipes appear by kind permission of Random House.

SARA PASTON-WILLIAMS acts as a consultant food historian to the National Trust as well as being the author of 14 cookery and food books, including **The Art of Dining — A History of Cooking and Eating**.

FÉLIX VELARDE is a native of Bilbao, Spain. A London resident for the last 27 years, he has for the last 11 years been the owner of **El Prado** restaurant in Parson's Green, West London, selected as a Critic's Choice in the **Time Out Eating & Drinking Guide**.

12 *Adieu ces bons vins de Lannoys*

The singer tells of his departure from Laon, lamenting, "I depart weighed down by my load of walnuts, for I cannot find beans or peas." The reference is not to the commonest peas available today, the green variety which are the fruit of pisum sativum *and which became fashionable in the 18th century. To get closer to a medieval taste, use split peas instead.*

The recipe, **Velouté aux pois gourmands trempé à la mie de pain aux épices,** *is closely based on one taken from* Le Ménagier de Paris *written by a French landowner of approximately 60 years of age for the benefit of his 15-year-old bride. The 'old' man not only offers his wife the benefit of his moral insights; he also gives essential practical instruction on how to handle servants and tradesmen, how to cope with the garden, and how to cook.*

SPLIT PEA SOUP THICKENED WITH SPICY BREAD AND SERVED WITH CONFIT CHICKEN

(Serves 6)

600 g (1-1/2 lb) split peas

4 thick slices of crusty bread (stale)

1 cooked confit chicken leg

1 large onion

1 clove of garlic

250 ml (1 cup) milk

2 cloves

1 star anis

Sprinkle of saffron

1 bay leaf

1/2 teaspoon of cinnamon

1 sprig thyme

1 sprig rosemary

Soak the peas in cold water overnight.
Chop and sweat the onion and garlic in a saucepan.
Add the split peas. Pour over half of the milk and
top up with water to just cover the peas. Season with
salt and pepper; allow to cook slowly for 3 hours or
until the peas are soft.

Blend the soup and pass through a sieve. In a
separate pan bring the remaining milk to a boil and
add all the spices and herbs. Allow this to infuse.
Add the bread and soak for 1 hour.

Remove the bread and spices; purée and strain
through a sieve. Add a little of the bread mixture to
the soup to thicken and flavour. (The thickness of
the soup should be of porridge-like consistency.)
Take the cooked chicken leg, remove the skin and
bones and flake in to soup bowls. Pour the soup over
the top and sprinkle with a little saffron for garnish.

Serve immediately.

JEAN-CHRISTOPHE NOVELLI

10 Donna di dentro

"Give me a little of that mazzacrocca!*"
Speculation has it that a* mazzacrocca *was a
long breadstick with a knob on the end and a
15th-century audience would have been fully
aware of the obscene connotations. This recipe
—* **Frittata di preboggion** *— by Rose Gray
and Ruth Rogers uses widely available Italian
bread in an innocent but delicious way.*

*Use a mixture of wild and cultivated greens —
dandelion, borage, sorrel, wild chicory, wild
rocket, cultivated rocket, small beet leaves
and/or Swiss chard leaves, mint and marjoram
leaves.*

FRITTATA WITH WILD LEAVES

(Serves 4)

1.5 kg (3-1/2 lb) green leaves,
washed (see note)
1/2 ciabatta loaf, bottom crust
removed, torn into 3–4 pieces
300 ml (1-1/3 cups) milk
Sea salt and black pepper,
freshly ground
150 g (6 oz) Parmesan cheese,
freshly grated
8 large, organic, free-range eggs
2 garlic cloves, peeled
Olive oil

Preheat the oven to 230° C / 450° F / Gas 8.
Soak the ciabatta in the milk for 20 minutes
until soft, then squeeze out excess milk and
chop finely.

Bring a large saucepan of water to boiling
point; add some salt, the garlic and then the
leaves. Cook for 5 minutes, drain well and
squeeze out all the water. Chop finely, using
a mezzaluna. Mix well with the chopped
bread, and season with salt, pepper and half
the Parmesan.

Break the eggs into a large bowl, season
generously, and beat. Stir in the greens
mixture. Use two 20-25 cm (8-10 inch)
frying pans with ovenproof handles. Heat 2
tablespoons olive oil in each pan, and when
hot, pour in half the mixture. Reduce the
heat and cook for a few minutes until just
set, but still quite runny. Scatter with the
remaining Parmesan, drizzle with olive oil,
and place in the hot oven. Leave until the
frittata becomes crisp at the edges and
slightly brown on top, a minute or two only.
Remove from the oven, loosen with a long
spatula, and place on warm serving plates.
Cut into wedges and serve.

ROSE GRAY AND RUTH ROGERS

3 Prenés l'abre /
Hé resveille toi Robin

This recipe comes from Le Ménagier de Paris, *an anonymous book written at the time of Chaucer and Guillaume de Machaut (also see note to Split Pea Soup recipe, page 80). The author, apparently a civil servant and landowner, advises on how to handle servants, how to manage a garden, and how to shop effectively in the Parisian markets, as well as assembling a comprehensive selection of recipes. These are sophisticated little pasties which would be perfect for al fresco dining or even the kind of picnic scene depicted in Adam de la Halle's* Le Jeu de Robin et Marion.

With two thirds of the pastry, line small deep patty pans. Chill. Preheat oven to 200° C / 400° F / Gas 5-6.

Trim off mushroom stalks. Using a sieve, dip mushrooms into boiling water for 2 minutes. Drain them, then pat dry and chop. Put them into a bowl and mix with the oil, cheese and seasonings. Fill the pastry-lined

MUSHROOM PASTIES (POPOVERS)

450 g (1 lb) short-crust pastry,
made with half butter, half lard

450 g (1 lb) mushrooms
(Paris or button mushrooms are best)

2 tablespoons olive oil

Salt and black pepper

55 g (2 oz) Cheddar cheese, grated

1/4 teaspoon dry mustard

1 egg, beaten

patty pans with the mixture. Roll out the remaining pastry and make lids. Seal with the beaten egg. Make a small cross in the centre of each lid.

Bake in the oven for 15-18 minutes. Serve warm.

CLARISSA DICKSON WRIGHT

17 *Ave color vini clari*

To mark this hymn of praise to the virtues of wine, a dish from Spain which utilises another closely related product of the grape — sherry. The recipe is entitled **Qui parla con se ffa esparaguat** *and can be found in the* Libre de sent soví *(Recipe No.117), an early 14th-century Spanish cookbook.*

ASPARAGUS IN SHERRY SAUCE

(Serves 4)

2 bunches medium-size asparagus
(20–24 sticks)

2 tablespoons plain flour

1 tablespoon olive oil

1 cup sherry (Fino or Manzanilla)

1 teaspoon dry tarragon leaves

1 teaspoon salt

Peel the asparagus, cutting off all dead and woody ends.

Bring some water to a boil in a large pot or pan (so that the asparagus is not bent while boiling) and blanch the asparagus. Reserve this water.

In a small pot, simmer the tarragon leaves and the sherry until reduced, then add two cups of the water used to blanch the asparagus and boil for 2-3 minutes.

Heat the olive oil in a frying pan and when hot add the flour, working it into a 'roux'; then add the boiling mixture of tarragon and sherry along with the salt, stirring to a creamy consistency. (More water can be added until the required texture is achieved.) Cook for about 10 minutes.

To serve, bring the remaining water up to a boil, put the asparagus back in, and finally cook to the required degree of crispness. At the same time, warm up the sauce ready for serving. Finger bowls may be necessary!

FÉLIX VELARDE

20 Von Eyren

The song celebrates the versatility of eggs and the recipe here is certainly unusual and imaginative. The creator of this dish — **Sic fac fritatem de pomeranciis** *— the German chef John [Johann] of Bockenheim, may well have known Guillaume Dufay (Track 12), as they were both in service to Pope Martin V in Rome around the year 1430. We can only speculate as to why this dish should be considered suitable for 'Pimps and Harlots' ("Et erit pro ruffianis et leccatricibus")!*

Sweet omelettes have fallen out of favour, which is a pity for they make excellent quick desserts. You can make this the suggested way with a fresh orange, adding grated zest to pep up the flavour, or use a spoonful of light marmalade instead. Ideal for leisurely breakfasts in bed, one omelette is enough for two to share.

ORANGE OMELETTE FOR PIMPS AND HARLOTS

(Serves 2)

1 sweet orange, or heaped tablespoon light orange marmalade

2 large or 3 medium free-range eggs

A good pinch of salt

1 tablespoon caster sugar (white table sugar)

1 teaspoon light olive oil

A good knob of butter

If using fresh orange, grate the zest finely,
then halve and squeeze out the juice.

Beat both juice and zest (or marmalade)
with the eggs, salt and sugar. Or if using
marmalade, beat that with the eggs instead.

Heat the oil and butter in a medium-size
omelette pan, about 20 cm (8 in.) in
diameter, until you can feel a good heat
rising. Make sure the butter doesn't burn.

Pour in the orange-y egg and swirl to coat
the base. Cook over medium heat, drawing
the lightly set egg mixture in towards the
centre with a fork or spatula to let the runny
egg slip over and cook. Repeat until the
whole mixture is lightly set. Hold the pan
over a warmed dinner plate and roll the
omelette on to the plate, or
erve folded over in half.

ROZ DENNY

Tortelloni with Ricotta, Lemon and Pine Kernels

(Serves 6)

Fresh pasta *(see page 90)*:

Semolina flour, for dusting

Sea salt and freshly ground pepper

Filling:

400 g (1 lb) buffalo ricotta cheese

1/3 nutmeg, freshly grated

150 g (5 oz) Parmesan, freshly grated

2 cm (1 inch) freshly peeled ginger root

75 g (2-1/2 oz) pine kernels,

lightly toasted

Peel of 1 lemon

Sauce:

Juice of 2 large lemons

200 ml (1 cup) double cream (heavy cream)

75 g (2-1/2 oz) softened butter

100 g (3-1/2 oz) Parmesan, freshly grated

11 *Canto di donne maestre di far cacio*

The lady cheese-makers from Chianti would unquestionably approve of this stunning pasta dish — **Tortelloni di ricotta, limone e pinoli** *— not least for the delicious use of other dairy products in the sauce.*

Prepare tortelloni dough *(see page 90)*.

To make the **filling**, break up the ricotta with a fork, and add the nutmeg, Parmesan, ginger and a generous dash of salt and pepper. Crush the pine kernels and carefully stir into the mixture. Finely chop the lemon peel and add to the ricotta. Stir in a little double cream if the mixture seems very stiff.

Dust your work surface with semolina flour. Divide the pasta dough into quarters. Roll the pieces out one at a time (use the finest setting on your pasta machine), to form long strips. Cut into 8-cm (3-inch) squares. Place a teaspoon of the filling in the centre of each square and fold over to form a triangle. Gently press to seal the dough around the filling. To form tortelloni, bend each triangle around your finger, joining the folded ends to slightly overlap, and press to seal, leaving the third point sticking up.

To make the **sauce**, heat the cream gently, then add the softened butter, lemon juice, Parmesan, salt and pepper. Keep warm over the gentlest possible heat.

Meanwhile, bring a large saucepan of water to a boil, season with 1 tablespoon of salt, and add the tortelloni. Simmer gently until the tortelloni are tender but firm to the bite, about 8-10 minutes. Drain, keeping a little of the pasta water. Place the tortelloni carefully into the thickened sauce. Add a little of the hot pasta water to liquefy if necessary, and serve with extra grated Parmesan.

(over)

Fresh Pasta:

500 g 'Tipo 00' pasta flour, plus extra flour for dusting

1 teaspoon sea salt

4 large organic free-range eggs, plus

6 large organic free-range egg yolks

50 g (1/4 cup) semolina flour, for dusting

Put the flour and salt into a food processor; add the eggs and egg yolks, and pulse-blend until the pasta begins to form a loose ball of dough. Knead the pasta dough on a flat surface, lightly dusted with the semolina and a little extra pasta flour, until the mixture is smooth, about 3 minutes. If the dough is stiff and very difficult to knead, return it to the processor and blend in another whole egg.

Cut the dough into 8 equal-sized pieces and briefly knead them into individual balls. Wrap each ball in cling film (Saran wrap) and allow to rest in fridge for at least 20 minutes (and up to 2 hours).

Prepare your pasta machine, setting it on the widest setting. Scatter the work surface with more flour, and pass each piece of pasta dough through the rollers ten times, folding the sheet into three each time; turn it by a quarter before passing it through the rollers again. This process introduces air into the dough and stretches it to develop the texture. After ten such folds at this setting the pasta should feel silky. Only then reduce the setting gradually down to fine.

ROSE GRAY AND RUTH ROGERS

2 *Chançonette / Ainc voir /*
A la cheminee / Par verité

This dish — **Potée de mouton et de bœuf au pain épices** — *is surely just what the singer of* A la cheminee *would have had in mind when he told of his wish for salt meat. The inspiration for this version of the dish is found in* Le Viandier de Guillaume Tirel, dit Taillevent. *Tirel was cook to the Kings Charles V (1364–80) and Charles VI (1380–1422) of France.*

Bring the stock to a boil. Add the shin, shoulder, and neck and all vegetables. Add the thyme, bay leaf, and rosemary. Season and allow to slowly simmer for 2 hours until the meat becomes extremely tender and flaky.

In a pan, roast all the spices and add a quarter of the cooking liquid. Allow to infuse, reduce by half and strain though a sieve.

Grate the bread, mix with the eggs to form a paste. Slowly add the reduced and infused cooking liquid until the sauce reaches thick consistency.

To serve, slice the different meats and arrange a small selection on each plate. Pour over a little of the cooking liquid and serve the spicy bread sauce on the side.

JEAN-CHRISTOPHE NOVELLI

BOILED BEEF AND MUTTON WITH SPICY BREAD SAUCE

(Serves 4)

1 shin of beef

1 shoulder of mutton

1 neck of mutton

3 onions

3 carrots

2 leeks

1 clove of garlic

2 litres (4 pints) of meat stock

Rosemary, thyme, bay leaf

4 slices of thick stale crusty bread

2 eggs

Cinnamon & clove

Juniper berries

Coriander seeds

Cardamom seeds

ROAST PORK WITH SPICED RED WINE

(Serves 4–6)

Allow at least 2 hours to marinate the meat.

1.35 kg (3 lb) loin of pork,
with skin and bone

2 medium-size onions, sliced

1 clove of garlic

1 bay leaf

1 level tablespoon fennel seeds, roughly
crushed in a pestle and mortar

Freshly milled black pepper

250 ml (1/2 pint) red wine

Freshly ground sea salt

25 g (1 oz) flour

About 250ml (1/2 pint) vegetable or
chicken stock

2 teaspoons quince or apple jelly

6 *Nowell, nowell: The boarës head*

This dish comes from the Curye on Inglysch *collection (see Spinach recipe on page 102) and was originally known as* **Cormarye**. *It was specifically designed with pork in mind, but the same marinating technique is worth using with boar, if your butcher can lay hands on one!*

Ask your butcher to chine the loin of pork, scoring the skin well and leaving the bone. Do not tie or roll the joint up with string.

Place the meat in a china or earthenware dish. Combine the onions, garlic, bay leaf, fennel seeds and black pepper with the red wine to make a marinade. Pour over the meat and leave to marinate for at least 2 hours.

Remove the joint, reserving the marinade; strain. Dry the skin of the pork with paper towels, then sit the joint upright, resting on the bones, in a shallow roasting pan. Sprinkle the scored surface of the skin generously with salt to give it a thick coating, then cook for 20 minutes in the oven at 240° C / 475° F / Gas 9. Lower the heat to 190° C / 375° F / Gas 5, and continue roasting for 1 hr and 10 min.

(To make sure that the meat is cooked, test with a skewer — the juices should run clear, not pink).

Place the pork on a serving dish and leave to rest in a warm place, while you make the gravy.

To make the **gravy**, remove most of the fat from the roasting pan. Stir the flour into the pan juices and cook for a few minutes. Pour in the strained marinade and continue to stir over moderate heat until smooth. Add the stock and allow to bubble for about 15 minutes until rich and glossy. Stir in about 2 teaspoons of quince or apple jelly and adjust the seasoning as necessary.

To serve, carve the meat into thick slices, including the crackling, and pour the red-wine sauce over it.

SARA PASTON-WILLIAMS

16 La tricotea & 18 Oy comamos y bebamos

With its discreet use of wine, this dish —
**Qui parla con se ffercexen capons e
gualines en ast ab fformatge** *— recreated
from the* Libre de sent soví *would appeal to the
revellers portrayed in these two Spanish songs.
You may also wish to experiment with the same
recipe for stuffing a goose, a dish traditionally
associated with St. Martin's Day celebrations
(***La Tricotea***).*

STUFFED CHICKEN
(Serves 4)

1 whole chicken

55 g (2 oz) cured ham,
diced (fatty bits preferable)

220 g (8 oz) minced pork

Chicken giblets, chopped

30 g (1 oz) parsley, finely chopped

1 medium-sized onion, chopped

1 clove of garlic, finely chopped

110 g (40 oz) grated cheese

1 hard-boiled egg, chopped

Olive oil

1 glass white wine

1 cup of water

Salt and pepper

Remove the giblets and bone the chicken.
Sprinkle with salt and pepper and leave
aside.

Put some olive oil in a saucepan with the
ham; when hot enough, add the onions and
garlic and fry until they turn gold in colour.
Add the minced pork, the giblets, parsley
and egg, stirring periodically until it is slowly
cooked into a 'paste.' Mix with the grated
cheese to form the final stuffing.

Place the stuffing inside the chicken, close
the opening with metal skewers, rub a little
oil on its skin, place it on a baking tray.
Add the water and roast in a pre-heated
oven, 180° C / 350° F / Gas 4, for 1 hour,
then pour the wine over the chicken,
increase the oven temperature to 190° C /
375° F / Gas 5, and cook for another
30 minutes.

Remove all skewers and let the chicken settle
for 15 minutes.

FÉLIX VELARDE

PHEASANT COOKED IN RED WINE WITH SPICES AND PARSLEY

(Serves 4)

2 prepared pheasants
(plucked and cleaned)
8 onions
1 head of celery
8 large carrots
1 head of garlic
250 g (10 oz) parsley, stalks and leaves
Clove
Cinnamon stick
1 bottle red wine
1 litre (2 pints) chicken stock
1 glass of port (optional)
1 bay leaf
Rosemary
Thyme
Juniper berries

13 Je ne vis onques

This song is known to have been sung at the Feast of the Pheasant *in 1454 and one must imagine that pheasant would have featured on the menu. This recipe —* **Marinade de faisan bourguignonne et sa persillade dernière minute** *— is based on one to be found in* Le recueil de Riom, *a collection compiled at least in part by M. Chavillat in 1466. A bottle of good Burgundian red wine would form the perfect accompaniment to this dish.*

Peel and prepare all vegetables, leaving them whole. Pan-fry all the vegetables until golden brown.

Brown the pheasants and place in a large saucepan or braising dish. Add the vegetables, the red wine, all the herbs and spices, and the parsley stalks. Pour in the chicken stock until the pheasants are completely covered in liquid. (A glass of port could be added for extra flavour.)

Cover with a lid and place in a moderate oven; braise for 1-1/2 hours or until the pheasant is completely cooked.

Remove from the oven, cut the pheasants into portions, chop the vegetables in half, and reduce the red-wine cooking liquor by half.

To serve, place the vegetables in the bottom of a dish, arrange the pheasant on top. Strain the cooking liquor and pour a little over the pheasant. Sprinkle with freshly chopped parsley and serve immediately.

JEAN-CHRISTOPHE NOVELLI

5 Apparuerunt apostolis v.
Spiritus Domini

*A very appropriate dish for the monks of
Fountains Abbey (Yorkshire), who brewed their
own ale and who would have been expected to
eschew meat in favour of fish on important
holy days. This recipe has been adapted from
an anonymous 15th-century cookbook (Laud
MS 533); any firm-fleshed white fish can be
used. For best results use good quality lagers
— they tend to be closer in texture to medieval
ales than modern bitters and stouts, the heavy
taste of which can sometimes mask the flavour
of the fish.*

Gently stew the onions with the saffron in
25 g (1 oz) butter for about 20 minutes, or
until very soft but not browned. Spoon them
into the bottom of a shallow ovenproof dish
into which the fish will just fit. Lay the fish
on top and season it well. Pour in the lager,
then cover the dish with foil. Bake in a
moderate oven, 180° C / 350° F / Gas 4,
for about 20 minutes until the fish is just
cooked through.

HADDOCK IN ALE
(Serves 4)

450 g (1 lb) thick piece of skinned
and filleted fresh haddock

2 onions, finely sliced

65 g (2-1/2 oz) butter

Generous pinch of saffron

Freshly milled black pepper

Freshly ground sea salt

250 ml (1/2 pint) lager

Flat-leaf (Italian) parsley,
roughly chopped

Strain off the liquor into a small pan and
reduce rapidly by fast boiling to intensify the
flavour. Divide the fish and onions between
4 shallow bowls (old-fashioned soup plates
are ideal) and keep warm.

Whisk the remaining butter into the liquor
and pour over the fish. Sprinkle with plenty
of parsley and then serve with fresh crusty
bread.

SARA PASTON-WILLIAMS

8 *Cacciando*

The markets of medieval Europe would have been brimming with fish, and this recipe — **Branzino arrosto con finocchio** *— combines one variety with a particular favourite of the times: fennel.*

Grilling the skin before baking gives the sea bass a distinctive and interesting flavour.

Preheat the oven to 190° C / 375° F / Gas 5. Preheat the grill.

Put half the fennel seeds and some salt and pepper inside the cavity of the fish, brush the skin with a little olive oil and grill for about 5–6 minutes on each side until the skin is lightly charred.

Place half the onion and lemon slices, parsley stalks, fennel slices and the remaining fennel seeds in a large ovenproof dish, lay the fish on top and cover with the remaining onion, lemon parsley and fennel. Pour over the lemon juice, olive oil and white wine, and bake in the oven for about 30 minutes, or until the flesh is firm to the touch.

Serve either hot or cold with **Green Sauce** (see next page)

ROSE GRAY AND RUTH ROGERS

ROASTED SEA BASS

(Serves 4 - 6)

1 2.25-kg (5-lb) sea bass,
scaled and cleaned but not filleted

2 tablespoons fennel seeds

Sea salt and
coarsely ground black pepper

2 red onions, peeled and sliced thinly

2 lemons, sliced

A few parsley stalks

2 fresh fennel bulbs, trimmed and sliced

Juice of 1 lemon

5 tablespoons olive oil

75 ml (1/3 cup) white wine

Green Sauce

1 large bunch flat-leaf (Italian) parsley

1 bunch fresh basil

A handful of fresh mint leaves

3 garlic cloves, peeled

100 g (4 oz) salted capers

100 g (4 oz) salted anchovies

2 tablespoons red wine vinegar

5 tablespoons extra virgin olive oil

1 tablespoon Dijon mustard

Sea salt

Freshly ground black pepper

8 *Cacciando*

An exceptionally popular sauce in medieval times often sold in markets in ready-made form, as is made clear by the text of the song. Rose Gray and Ruth Rogers' version — **Salsa verde** *— uses many ingredients that feature in the street-vendors cries.*

If using a food processor, pulse-chop the parsley, basil, mint, garlic, capers, and anchovies until roughly blended. Transfer to a large bowl and add the vinegar. Slowly pour in the olive oil, stirring constantly, and finally add the mustard. Check for seasoning.

This sauce may also be prepared by hand on a board, preferably using a *mezzaluna*.

ROSE GRAY AND RUTH ROGERS

FRIED SPINACH

450 g (1 lb) fresh spinach
1 tablespoon olive oil
Sea salt
Freshly ground black pepper
Freshly grated nutmeg
A pinch of ground ginger

This simple recipe for spinach has been adapted from the Curye on Inglysch *collection, compiled by Royal command for use by the chefs at the court of King Richard II (ruled 1377–99). According to the chronicler Holinshed, Richard had 2,000 cooks in his service — possibly a slight exaggeration!*

Pick over the spinach leaves and wash in at least two changes of water to remove any grit. Remove all the central tough stalks and tear the leaves into manageable pieces, unless they are small, in which case leave them whole. Drain well.

Bring a pan of salted water to a boil and drop in the spinach leaves. Bring back to a boil, then strain immediately through a colander to get as much moisture out of the spinach as possible.

In a clean pan, heat the olive oil until smoking, then add the spinach. Cook over high heat for a few minutes until the spinach is dry, then season with salt, pepper, nutmeg and ginger.

SARA PASTON-WILLIAMS

This dish was a great favourite in medieval times but the recipe probably dates originally from the Roman era. Leeks are an ancient vegetable which grew well all over Europe and were especially prized in France, Italy and Spain. The beetroot was much prized at the dinner table for its clear rich purple colour as well as its taste. This dish with its reduced sauce could be easily eaten with fingers or a spoon.

Grind together the cumin and coriander. Heat the stock and add the raisins and spices. Put in the vegetables, add salt and simmer until the vegetables are tender (about 25 minutes). Remove the vegetables from the sauce to a warm dish. Reduce the sauce, adding a little flour to thicken and a dash of oil and vinegar. Pour over vegetables and serve.

CLARISSA DICKSON WRIGHT

LEEKS AND BEETROOT IN RAISIN SAUCE

2 leeks, sliced.

225 g (1/2 lb) young whole beetroots

1 teaspoon coriander seeds

1/4 teaspoon cumin seeds

55 g (2 oz) raisins

600 ml (2-2/3 cups) vegetable stock

Olive oil

White wine vinegar

Flour

Salt

With the Burgundian fondness for pies and pastries this recipe — **Tourte aux poires et son flan croustillant** — *might even have been one of the 'fine dishes' served at the party hosted by the composers Morton and Hayne to which the song text makes reference. From Le Viandier de Guillaume Tirel, dit Taillevent.*

Slice the pears into quarters.

Bake 'blind' your pastry shell for 20 minutes at 200° C / 400° F / Gas 5–6.

Spread the frangipane in the bottom of the pastry shell; top with pear quarters.

Mix together the egg, double cream, sugar, saffron and a splash of rum; pour over the pears. Bake in a warm oven, approximately 150° C / 300° F / Gas 2, for 1 hour and 15 minutes, until the pears are soft and the egg mixture has set.

Crumb together the butter, flour and brown sugar and sprinkle over the tart. Return the tart to the hot oven or bake under a grill until the topping is golden brown.

Serve immediately

JEAN-CHRISTOPHE NOVELLI

PEAR TART
(Serves 6)

3 ripe pears, peeled and cored

1 sweet short-crust pastry shell

250 g (9 oz) frangipane*

150 g (5 oz) caster sugar
(white table sugar)

Saffron

100 g (3-1/2 oz) butter

100 g (3-1/2 oz) flour

1 egg

100 ml (1/2 cup) double cream
(heavy cream)

Rum (optional)

50 g (2 oz) brown sugar

commonly made from almond paste, butter, sugar, flour and egg.

Saffron, taken from the stamen of the crocus, was beloved by people in the Middle Ages, especially for its vivid colour.

This is a sophisticated dish: saffron was and is horrendously expensive and baking in the 15th century was no easy matter, requiring as it did a brick oven heated by fire to raise the bricks to the right temperature. The fire was then raked out and baking could begin. Because of the difficulty, yeasted cakes with a shorter cooking time were much favoured. The finest sultanas and raisins came from Cyprus and the mace in question was the herb mace.

SAFFRON CAKE

450 g (1 lb) plain flour

12.5 g (1/2 oz) yeast

110 g (1/4 lb) butter

55 g (2 oz) caster sugar
(white table sugar)

55 g (2 oz) each sultanas and currants

150 ml (2/3 cup) milk

1 teaspoon salt

1 teaspoon each powdered mace
and mixed spice

1/2 teaspoon saffron filaments

For glazing:

2 tablespoons milk, mixed with

1 tablespoon sugar

To prepare the saffron and the yeast, take half the milk and heat to boiling point. Put the saffron filaments on a dish and place it in a hot oven for 5 minutes. Crumble into a cup; pour over a little hot milk and leave to infuse. Pour the remaining hot milk, which by now will be lukewarm, over the yeast and mix to a cream.

Put the flour, sugar and salt in a warmed bowl. Sprinkle in the dry spices and stir in the creamed yeast. Now mix in the softened butter with your hands, and when it is well mixed add the saffron infusion and the remainder of the milk. The dough should be soft but not runny. Mix in the fruit, cover and leave to rise for about 2 hours. When it has doubled in volume, knock it down lightly. Sprinkle with flour, transfer to a buttered tin, and leave to rise for a second time. It is a slow-rising dough and will take a minimum of 45 minutes to 1 hour to return to life and reach almost to the top of the tin.

Bake in the centre of the oven at 200° C / 400° F / Gas 5-6, for 15 minutes. Move to a lower shelf and cook for a further 15 minutes. Remove from oven, glaze, and leave for 15 minutes before turning out.

Although saffron cake is best enjoyed when freshly cooked, it can be reheated in a very low oven. It is a subtle accompaniment to a sweet Sauternes, a dessert wine, or a glass of Madeira.

CLARISSA DICKSON WRIGHT

1 *In pauperatis predio*

The opening song provides a lovely image of St. Francis tending his vineyards and fig trees and this recipe — **Gâteau de pain bouilli au lait d'amande safrané et son croustillant de figues et de raisins** *— employs the produce of both. Also, it is impossible to overstate the importance of almonds in medieval cooking; they were used both in their natural state and to form a 'milk,' which could be used in all manner of dishes. This recipe is also taken from* Le Viandier de Guillaume Tirel, dit Taillevent.

BREAD, ALMOND AND SAFFRON PUDDING WITH A FIG AND RAISIN CRUST

(Serves 4)

8 thick slices of brioche (or egg bread)

300 ml (1-1/3 cups) of milk

130 g (2/3 cup) caster sugar
(white table sugar)

100 g (3-1/2 oz) flaked almonds

4 dried figs, diced

100 g (3-1/2 oz) raisins

1 tablespoon brown sugar

40 g (1-1/2 oz) butter

1 measure of rum

1 teaspoon of saffron

1 teaspoon of ground cinnamon

2 eggs, plus 1 yolk

FOR STOCK SYRUP:

100 g (3-1/2 oz) caster sugar

300 ml (1-1/3 cups) water

To prepare the stock syrup, stir and dissolve the caster sugar in a pan of water; bring to a boil. Add the raisins, almonds, figs and the rum and remove from the heat. Cover with cling film (Saran wrap) and leave to infuse for at least 2 hours.

Spoon out and drain half of the figs and raisins from the pan and reserve; reduce the remaining mixture by half to produce a thick syrup and set aside.

Pre-heat the oven to 180° C / 350° F / Gas 4. Spread the brioche slices thinly with butter on both sides and cut into cubes. Put into a bowl with half the drained raisins and figs, the cinnamon and the brown sugar.

Heat the milk and the saffron in a pan and bring to a boil. In another bowl beat together the eggs, egg yolks, and the caster sugar, until pale. Pour the milk slowly over the eggs-and-sugar mixture, beating all the time until smooth. Pass through a sieve and add to the bowl containing the brioche and fruit. Mix well to combine.

Butter your 4 moulds* and line with the reserved raisins and figs. Fill with the brioche mixture divided evenly between them. Bake in a bain-marie in the preheated oven for 30 minutes until golden brown and well risen.

To serve, turn the puddings out of their moulds and pour a little of the raisin-and-fig syrup over the top. Cream or ice cream could be added for modern palates.

JEAN-CHRISTOPHE NOVELLI

*small china moulds, ramekins or tea cups

22 *Trinkt und singt*

Given the German fondness for beer and apples, it seems only natural to link this song with this dish. The recipe — **Pachen Oppheln** *— has been adapted from a German manuscript now at the Biblioteca del Seminario Maggiore, Bressanone, Italy.*

Few modern kitchens will have a wooden spindle with a knob as originally demanded in this recipe, although baking on a spindle is preserved in Germany with the Baumkuchen, *or 'Treecake' made by pouring a cake batter on a horizontal spit revolving in front of an open fire. Nevertheless one is able to recapture the essence of this recipe in one of two ways: either wrapping the apple-and-pear filling in a sweet pastry for an oven dumpling, or dipping fruit slices sandwiched with a purée into a thick batter which is then deep-fried into fritters.*

BAKED APPLES FOR A DRINKING SESSION

(Serves 4–6)

4 medium-size firm pears

e.g. Comice or Conference

5 dessert apples

About 100 g (3-1/4 oz) sweet seedless

grapes (green)

50 g (1/4 cup) caster sugar

(white table sugar)

A good pinch of saffron filaments, or

1/2 teaspoon ground mixed spice

FOR DUMPLINGS:

500 g (1 lb 2 oz) sweet short-crust pastry,

thawed if frozen,

rolled & cut into squares

1 egg yolk, beaten with 2 teaspoons water

(for glaze)

Thick cream (optional)

(Fritter batter — see page 112)

Peel, core and chop the pears and 1 of the apples. Place both fruits in a saucepan with the grapes, 50 g (1/4 cup) sugar and crushed saffron or mixed spice. Add a splash or two of water if necessary. Heat until the fruits sizzle, then cover and cook gently for about 12 minutes until pulpy and soft. Uncover and cook for another 5 minutes to reduce down to a thick purée. Beat well with a wooden spoon until smooth. Set aside to cool completely and chill.

Using an apple corer, remove the cores from the 4 remaining apples. Peel off the skin, cut the apples horizontally into thin slices.

If making the **dumplings**, divide the pastry into four then roll each portion out to a 22-cm (9-inch) square. Brush the edges with some egg glaze. Now spread the fruit purée in between the apple slices, reassembling the apple. It doesn't matter if it is a bit messy. Make the filling as thick as you can without it oozing out.

Place each layered apple in the centre of a pastry square. Wrap the sides up all round the apple and press the edges together firmly so they stick into a rosette. Trim the top to neaten. Repeat with the remaining apples, filling and pastry. Place each dumpling on a non-stick baking sheet. Chill for at least half an hour to firm.

Meanwhile, heat the oven to 200° C / 400° F / Gas 6. Brush the outside of each dumpling with more egg glaze and bake for 20 minutes, turning before the pastry burns. Then reduce the heat to 180° C / 350° F / Gas 4, and bake for another 10 minutes.

Cool the dumplings for 15 minutes at least before serving. Good with lovely thick cream.
(over)

For fritter batter:
125 g (1 cup) plain flour
50 g (1/4 cup) caster sugar,
plus extra for serving
2 eggs, 1 separated into yolk and white
1 tablespoon sunflower oil or
melted butter
150 ml (2/3 cup) milk
Oil, for deep-frying

If making **fritters**, beat the batter ingredients in a food processor to a thick batter, or beat in a bowl with a metal balloon whisk. Get the fruits ready. Fill a pan or wok a third full of oil, heat to about 180° C / 350° F / Gas 4, or until a cube of day-old white bread browns in 30 seconds.

Sandwich just two apple slices at a time with filling. Dip quickly into the batter and lower gently into the fat. Cook about 3 at a time for 2-3 minutes until golden-brown and crisp. Drain on paper towels and keep warm, uncovered so they remain crisp. Dredge with caster sugar to serve.

ROZ DENNY

2 Chançonette / Ainc voir / A la cheminee / Par verité

C'est sûrement à un plat de ce genre que l'auteur de « A la cheminee » pensait lorsqu'il dit avoir envie de « chair salée ». Cette recette est très proche de celle qui figure dans Le Viandier de Guillaume Tirel, dit Taillevent. Tirel fut le cuisinier des rois de France Charles V (1364–1380) et Charles VI (1380–1422).

Préparation : Porter le bouillon à ébullition. Ajouter le jarret, l'épaule, le collier et tous les légumes. Ajouter le thym, la feuille de laurier et le romarin. Assaisonner et laisser mijoter pendant 2 heures jusqu'à ce que la viande soit bien tendre. Griller les épices dans un poêlon, ajouter un quart du liquide de cuisson. Faire réduire de moitié à feu doux puis tamiser. Râper le pain, mélanger avec les œufs de façon homogène. Ajouter lentement l'infusion tamisée jusqu'à obtenir la consistance d'une sauce au pain.

Présentation : Découper les différentes viandes et en garnir chaque assiette. Verser un peu de bouillon. Servir la sauce au pain épicée à part.

JEAN-CHRISTOPHE NOVELLI

POTÉE DE MOUTON ET DE BŒUF À LA SAUCE AU PAIN ÉPICÉE

(Ingrédients pour 4 personnes)

1 jarret de bœuf

1 épaule de mouton

1 collier de mouton

3 oignons

3 carottes

2 poireaux

1 gousse d'ail

2 litres de bouillon de viande

romarin, thym, 1 feuille de laurier

4 tranches de gros pain rassis

2 œufs

cannelle

clous de girofle

baies de genièvre

graines de coriandre

graines de cardamome

Pour obtenir copie d'autres recettes traduites en français ou pour en savoir plus sur leurs auteurs, rendez-vous sur le **www.harmoniamundi.com**

ESSEN, TRINKEN UND SINGEN
Musik und Tafelfreuden im Europa der Renaissance

Die Speisen

Wer sich mit mittelalterlichen Kochrezepten befasst, wird sehr schnell feststellen, wie einfallsreich und erfinderisch die mittelalterlichen Küchenchefs zu Werke gingen. Das sollte einen freilich nicht allzu sehr verwundern, war doch die Epoche, in der die hier eingespielten Musikstücke entstanden, eine Zeit umwälzender Neuerungen auf dem Gebiet der Kochkunst. Die Erschließung neuer Handelswege in den Orient bescherte den Köchen eine Fülle unbekannter exotischer Gewürze, die mit einem über-wältigenden Angebot inländischer Erzeugnisse kombiniert werden konnten. Auf den Märkten gab es die frischesten landwirtschaftlichen Produkte im Überfluss: Gemüse, Salate, Fleisch, Fisch, Milchprodukte, Mehl und Getreide, Würzsaucen, Kräuter — im Text von Cacciando (Track 8) ist dies eindrucksvoll belegt. Und obendrein waren alle diese Waren reine Naturprodukte!

20 Von Eyren

Das Lied rühmt die vielseitige kulinarische Verwendbarkeit der Eier, nennt aber nicht das hier vorgestellte recht ungewöhnliche und phantasievolle Rezept. Der deutsche Küchenchef Johann von Bockenheim, der diese Speise erfunden hat, dürfte Guillaume Dufay (Track 12) sehr gut gekannt haben, denn beide standen um 1430 in Diensten von Papst Martin V. in Rom. Weshalb diese Speise gerade für "Kuppler und Dirnen" ("Et erit pro ruffianis et leccatricibus", wie es am Ende des Originalrezepts heißt), so besonders zuträglich sein soll, bleibt unerfindlich, darüber kann man nur Vermutungen anstellen!

Süße Omeletts waren im letzten Jahrhundert nicht mehr so gefragt; das ist schade, denn sie sind hervorragend als Dessert geeignet und schnell zubereitet. Sie können, wie hier angegeben, frische Orangen verwenden und den Geschmack mit abgeriebener Orangen-schale verfeinern, oder die Orangen auch durch einen Löffel helle Orangenmarmelade ersetzen. Ideal für das gemütliche Frühstück im Bett; ein Omelett ist ausreichend für zwei Personen.

ORANGEN-OMELETT FÜR
KUPPLER UND DIRNEN

Sic fac fritatem de pomeranciis

(für 2 Personen)

1 frische Orange oder ein gehäufter
Esslöffel helle Orangenmarmelade

2 große oder 3 mittelgroße
Freiland-Eier

1 gute Prise Salz

1 Esslöffel Puderzucker

1 Teelöffel helles Olivenöl

1 nicht zu kleines Stückchen Butter

*Wünschen Sie weitere Rezepte in deutscher
Übersetzung, die Sie ausdrucken können, oder
biographische Informationen über die einzelnen
Küchenchefs? Dann besuchen Sie bitte unsere
Website* www.harmoniamundi.com

Wenn Sie das Omelett mit frischer Orange
zubereiten, die Schale sorgfältig abreiben, die
Orange halbieren und den Saft auspressen.
Den Saft und die Orangenschale mit den
Eiern, Salz und Zucker verrühren. Oder,
wenn Sie Marmelade verwenden, diese mit
den Eiern verrühren.

Öl und Butter in einer mittelgroßen
Omelett-Pfanne (etwa 20 cm Durchmesser)
erhitzen, bis Sie ausreichende Hitze auf-
steigen fühlen. Achten Sie darauf, dass die
Butter nicht braun wird.

Das Orangen-Ei-Gemisch in die Pfanne
gießen und durch Schwenken gleichmäßig
verteilen. Bei mittlerer Hitze backen; sobald
die Masse zu stocken beginnt, mit einer
Gabel oder einem Kochlöffel vorsichtig zur
Pfannenmitte hin schieben, so dass das noch
flüssige Ei überlaufen und stocken kann.
So lange weiter erhitzen, bis die Masse
einigermaßen fest geworden ist. Die Pfanne
über einen vorgewärmten Teller halten und
das Omelett darauf gleiten lassen oder mit
einem Pfannenwender halb überklappen und
auf den Teller gleiten lassen. Mit zwei Gabeln
servieren.

ROZ DENNY

COMIDA, VINO Y CANCIÓN
Música y celebración en la Europa renacentista

La comida

Sólo una breve mirada a una colección de recetas medievales pone de manifiesto la ingenuidad y las habilidades creativas de los *chefs* de la época. Pero esto no debería ser una sorpresa. El periodo de cubre esta antología musical fue de gran innovación en el mundo culinario. Con la apertura de las rutas de comercio hacia el este, los cocineros pudieron acceder a especias nuevas y exóticas. Éstas podían combinarse con una asombrosa colección de productos existentes. En los mercados abundaba el género más fresco: vegetales, lechugas, carne, pescado, productos del día, grano y harina, salsas, hierbas — el texto de **Cacciando** (pista 8) da testimonio de ello. Más aún, todo era orgánico.

Los platos incluidos en esta antología se han tomado todos de recetas que pueden encontrarse en colecciones de toda Europa desde los siglos XIV y XV. Algunas, como las de Jean-Christophe Novelli, requerían comenzar desde un tablero de dibujo, pero otras apenas necesitaban adaptación. (La sección italiana por Rose Gray y Ruth Rogers sólo necesitó unos cambios de recetas que hoy se encuentran en el River Cafe). Nuestros chefs 'modernos' han combinado, como hubieran hecho sus colegas medievales, los textos con su propia imaginación, pero las técnicas de cocinar serían reconocibles para sus antecesores. El vino o la cerveza serían el acompañamiento más adecuado para estos platos — después de todo, seguramente eran más sanos que el agua en la Edad Media. Y para acercarse algo más a una 'experiencia' medieval le sugerimos que utilice sólo cucharas y cuchillos. Los tenedores no se encuentran en las fuentes inglesas antes de 1463 y no fueron de uso común hasta el siglo XVII — pero tenga en cuenta que recurrir al uso de las manos se hubiera considerado una falta de modales.

Para una copia impresa del comentario, otras recetas traducidas al español, o información sobre cada cocinero, por favor visite **www.harmoniamundi.com**

17 Ave color vini clari

Para acompañar este himno a las virtudes del vino, un plato de España que utiliza otro producto derivado de la uva, el jerez. La receta está intitulada 'Qui parla con se ffa esparaguat' [Que habla de cómo se hace el esparragado (guiso de espárragos)] y puede encontrarse en el Libre de sent soví *(receta nº117), un recetario español de comienzos del siglo XIV.*

ESPÁRRAGOS EN SALSA DE JEREZ

(Para cuatro personas)

2 manojos de espárragos de tamaño medio (20-24 tallos)

2 cucharadas de harina

1 cucharada de aceite de oliva

1 taza de jerez (fino o manzanilla)

1 cucharadita de hojas secas de estragón

1 cucharadita de sal

Se lleva agua a ebullición en una olla o cacerola alargada, de forma que los espárragos no se doblen al cocer, y se blanquean los espárragos dejándolos crujientes. Reservar el agua.

En una cacerola pequeña se ponen las hojas de estragón y el jerez, y se reduce. Se añaden entonces dos tazas del agua de cocer los espárragos y se deja hervir durante dos o tres minutos.

Se calienta el aceite de oliva en una sartén. Una vez caliente se añade la harina, trabajándola hasta obtener una pasta. Se añade entonces la mezcla hirviendo de estragón y jerez, junto con la sal hasta conseguir una consistencia cremosa. (Puede añadirse más agua hasta conseguir el punto deseado.) Cocer durante unos diez minutos. La salsa está lista.

Para servir, llevar el agua restante a ebullición, poner en ella los espárragos y cocerlos hasta el punto deseado. Calentar al mismo tiempo la salsa y presentarla en una salsera. Pueden ser necesarios lavafrutas.

ROZ DENNY

MANGIARE, BERE, E CANTARE
Musica e banchetti nel Rinascimento

La *cucina*

Sfogliando una collezione di ricette medioevali notiamo subito la creatività dei cuochi—e ciò non ci sorprende: questi furono secoli di scoperte, anche culinarie. Nuove spezie venivano dall'oriente, ed erano abbinate ai prodotti indigeni: verdure, carni, pesce, latticini, grano, farina—'Cacciando' (CD, n. 8) ne dà testimonianza—tutti prodotti organici!

Però non tutti mangiavano 'bene'; ciò dipendeva dal ceto sociale. C'erano le grandi feste per pochi privilegiati, che mangiavano e bevevano in quantità oscene; c'erano anche coloro che sopravvivevano di poco e che, essendo malnutriti, erano suscettibili a tante malattie; ma la maggioranza viveva certamente un compromesso tra questi estremi. I cuochi medioevali conoscevano gli effetti salutari dei cibi, e usavano fantasiosamente gli ingredienti disponibili nelle varie stagioni.

Ciò si capisce dalle loro raccolte di ricette. Molte provengono dalle cucine privilegiate, ma tra i piatti raffinati se ne trovano anche di semplici: gli autori propongono idee da adattare a varie occasioni. Danno istruzioni piuttosto imprecise, che stimolavano la memoria presupponendo che il cuoco già conoscesse le tecniche essenziali e sapesse scegliere i sapori più indicati per la situazione. Le ricette erano anche raggruppate secondo criteri per noi strani: piatti per ammalati, organizzati secondo le varie malattie, oppure per i religiosi che dovevano seguire rigide diete.

Le nostre ricette provengono da fonti del '300 e '400. Alcune, come quelle di Jean-Cristophe Novelli, sono state 'riscritte' di sana pianta; altre, come quelle italiane, sono state modificate solo minimamente. I cuochi 'moderni', come i loro predecessori, hanno dovuto agire di fantasia, ma le tecniche e gli ingredienti sono quelli del medioevo. Accompagnate questi piatti con vino o birra—certamente allora erano più salubri dell'acqua. E se volete sentirvi veramente partecipi di una esperienza medioevale, provate a usare solo coltelli e cucchiai—della forchetta non si parla fino al 1463, e entra in uso comune solo nel '600. E ricordatevi che chi usava le dita era considerato maleducato!

Per la traduzione in italiano del saggio introduttivo, dei cenni biografici riguardanti ciascun cuoco, e di tutte le ricette, visitate **www.harmoniamundi.com**

Nel medioevo questo piatto era favorito in Francia, Italia, e Spagna, ma la ricetta risale probabilmente a Roma antica, quando i porri erano già coltivati in tutta Europa. Le barbabietole erano particolarmente prezzate sia per la purezza e intensità del colore rosso-violaceo sia per il sapore. La salsa è densa, per cui si può mangiare con il cucchiaio o con le dita.

Macina insieme il comino e il coriandolo. Scalda il brodo e aggiungi l'uva passa e le spezie. Aggiungi le verdure e il sale, e fai bollire lentamente fino a quando le verdure diventano tenere. Metti le verdure in un piatto caldo, e fai ridurre la salsa, aggiungendo l'olio e l'aceto, e della farina per addensirla. Versala sulle verdure e servi.

CLARISSA DICKSON-WRIGHT

PORRI E BARBABIETOLE INTERE BRASATI CON UVA SECCA

2 porri, affettati

225 g. di barbabietole novelle

1 cucchiaino di semi di coriandolo

1/4 di cucchiaino di comino

55 g. di uva passa

600 ml di brodo di verdure

Olio d'oliva

Aceto di vino bianco

Farina

Sale

ACKNOWLEDGMENTS

Front cover: *Peasant Wedding* (Bauernhochzeit), 1568 (panel) by
Pieter the Elder Brueghel (c.1515–69), Kunsthistorisches Museum,
Vienna, Austria/Bridgeman Art Library.
Page 13: Capital V; monk drinking. Sloane 2435 f44v, by permission of The British Library.
Page 77: A Medieval Kitchen (woodcut) by Italian School (16th century)
Private Collection/Bridgeman Art Library.

Woodcut Illustrations: Dover Publications.

The performing editions used in this recording were prepared by Daniel Leech-Wilkinson,
Wyndham Thomas, Margaret Bent, David Fallows, Tess Knighton and
Clifford Bartlett from original sources.

All texts and translations © harmonia mundi usa

℗ © 2001 **harmonia mundi usa**
2037 Granville Avenue, Los Angeles, CA 90025

Recorded September 1–4, 1999 at St. Osdag Kirche,
Neustadt - Mandelsloh, Lower Saxony (Germany).
Executive Producer **harmonia mundi usa**: Robina G. Young
Executive Producer: David R. Murray
Recording Producer: Oliver Rogalla
Balance Engineer: Gregor Zielinsky / Recording Engineer: Matthias Schwab
Pronunciation Adviser: Alison Wray
English Translations: Leofranc Holford-Strevens
Design: Karin Elsener